A Newbies Guide to iPad Pro, iPad Air 2 and iPad Mini 3

(Or Any iPad with iOS 9)

Minute Help Press

www.minutehelp.com

Cover Image © kelly marken- Fotolia.com

i

Table of Contents

Introduction

Welcome to the world of the Apple iPad! The slim, elegant device in your hands has revolutionized personal computing and introduced entirely new ways of seeking, consuming and sharing content. iPad is also incredibly intuitive – with a handful of buttons and a few gestures, you'll gain access to a world of information, music, video, games, connectivity, productivity and more. In other words, you're in for a tasty technological treat.

If you're new to the Apple family of mobile devices (iPhone, iPod, iPad), or if you're new to mobile computing altogether, this guide will help you get the most out of your new iPad and iOS 9. Even if you've used older versions of iPad or iOS, you'll find plenty of new ways to learn, work, play and share with your new iPad running iOS 9. We'll show you how to set up and customize your iPad, use all of the preinstalled apps like an expert, keep your iPad healthy and happy, and discover some of the best free and nearly free third party apps available in the Apple App Store. Along the way, we'll give you plenty of easy-to-follow instructions, screenshots, tips and tricks that will have you tapping, swiping, syncing and sharing like a pro in no time!

About This Guide

This guide is designed for novices and advanced iPad/iOS users alike. The tips and instructions here are tailored to the three most recent iPad models – iPad Pro, iPad Air 2, and iPad Mini 4 - and iOS 9, but you'll find plenty of relevant information for older iPad models and older versions of the iOS software.

We've broken things down into six major parts. **Part 1: Meet Your iPad** will help you unpack the box, learn how to interact with your iPad, and breeze through the set up process. **Part 2: Getting to Know Your iPad** will introduce you to the basic features and navigational system of the device. **Part 3: Mastering Your Preinstalled Apps** will walk you through the twenty preinstalled apps in detail to help you master what's available right out of the box. **Part 4: Making It Your Own** guides you through customization and personalization. **Part 5: Maintenance and Security** will help you keep your iPad healthy and safe. Finally, **Part 6: Must-Have Apps for Your iPad** includes a list of 49 of our favorite apps – we hope you like them as much as we do!

There's a lot of information here, and don't feel like you need to absorb it all at once. Think of this guide as a friendly support system for you as you learn to use and enjoy this incredible technology. If you're new to iPad or to iOS, start by reading through Parts 1 and 2. This should get you on your feet. Be sure to look at Part 5 to learn how to care for your new iPad. You may want to use Parts 3, 4, and 6 as reference material. Rather than reading them straight through from start to finish, browse the table of contents for the information most helpful to you. These chapters will also be helpful for experienced users who want to get the most out of iPad and iOS 9.

Few devices are as painless to use as the iPad – have fun and enjoy the journey! Now let's get started.

About iPad and iOS 9

The Apple iPad is a tablet that can be used without any of the standard peripherals you need to get the most out of a PC – no need to attach speakers, microphones, mice, or keyboards. If you've used an iPhone or an iPod Touch, you're already familiar with the dazzling touchscreen technology that makes the iPad so much fun to use. The keyboard appears on the touchscreen when needed, and instead of a mouse, you'll use your finger(s) to interact with the device. iPad can also register more than one simultaneous touch, which allows users to double tap and use other multi-touch gestures. iPad also includes a camera capable of taking still images and video, a built-in microphone and speaker, and Location Services (services that use cellular and wireless data and GPS to determine your iPad's location).

As of October 2015, seven versions of the Apple iPad have been released. The first generation model was released in 2010. The second generation, the iPad 2, followed in 2011, and added a camera, an improved processor, and supported FaceTime (more on this later). In 2012, Apple released the third generation iPad, sometimes referred to as an iPad 3, but officially named "the new iPad." The new iPad included a stunning Retina display with nearly four times the total number of pixels in an iPad 2 screen. Shortly afterward, Apple released a fourth generation iPad with some hardware improvements and a lightning dock, along with the first generation of the iPad Mini – a smaller, more affordable version of Apple's tablet.

In 2013, Apple released the iPad Air – a lighter, more powerful design with all of the features of the original iPad form factor and then some. In October 2014, Apple announced the iPad Air 2, complete with Touch ID sensor, the M8 motion coprocessor, and improved performance. The iPad Mini also continued developing and is now in its fourth generation. The Mini 4 includes the A8 processor and M8 motion coprocessor, as well as a Retina display and Touch ID.

In September 2015, Apple announced the most sophisticated iPad yet – the iPad Pro. The iPad Pro is larger than the standard iPad model. It's 12 inches tall, compared to the 9.4 inch tall iPad Air and the 8 inch tall Mini. That includes a 12.9-inch screen (compared to 9.7 on the iPad Air and 7.9 on the Mini), with a glorious 2732 x 2048 resolution. There's more to the iPad Pro than its size, though. Inside, it includes the newest, fastest, most powerful Apple processor, the A9 chip, and the latest iteration of Apple's legendary motion co-processor, the M9.

iPad Pro, iPad Air 2 and iPad Mini 4 can all be purchased in cellular-enabled and Wi-Fi only models. A 3G model can connect to a 3G network (and to 4G LTE, where available), meaning you can access the Internet almost anywhere. However, 3G models require a data plan from a wireless carrier, meaning there will be a monthly charge involved. The Wi-Fi only iPad can connect to standard wireless networks (like the one you may have set up in your home) for free, but you'll be limited to locations where Wi-Fi is available. Note that only the 128 GB iPad Pro can be purchased as Wi-Fi and Cellular compatible.

So what exactly is an iPad good for? At first glance, it might look like a giant iPhone that can't make standard phone calls or a laptop without a keyboard, but you'll be amazed at how soon you'll be wondering how you ever lived without it. The iPad is a handheld television, an intuitive ereader, a personal gaming system, a portable magazine rack, a gateway to the Internet, a music repository, a social media connection, and much, much more. You can take photos and video, draw, create documents, spreadsheets, and presentations, and improve yourself with flashcards and other learning systems. Your iPad is portable enough to go anywhere with you, and so can your entire social network, since iPad supports deep integration with both Twitter and Facebook.

The software that supports all of this activity is called iOS 9. iOS 9 is the most current version of iOS, and it runs on iPad Pro, iPad 2 and newer, iPad Air 1 and 2, all iPad Mini models, iPhone 4S and newer, and iPod Touch fifth generation and newer. iOS is the Apple mobile operating system, and iOS 9 is its ninth major version release. We'll refer to iOS 9 quite a bit throughout this guide, so you'll want to understand what we're talking about. Without getting too far into specifics, think of your digital content as a really exotic pet, and the operating system as the specialized habitat that it lives in. Now, just like you wouldn't put a hamster wheel in a fish tank, you wouldn't install a Windows program on an iOS 9 device - in fact, you can't. When you're setting up your iOS 9 "habitat," you'll be populating it with apps (also known as programs to Windows users) designed especially for iOS devices. Fortunately, iOS devices make it very easy to find iOS apps. They're all located in the Apple App Store, and all you'll need is an Apple ID and a finger to access them.

Ready to see what all the fuss is about? Let's get your iPad out of the box and into your hands!

Part 1: Meet Your iPad

We're going to start at the very beginning by introducing some of the key concepts you'll need to get started, including what's included in the box, the buttons and hardware on your iPad, and the ways you'll interact with your device, including actions and typing. Then we'll walk through the setup process. You may find yourself referring back to the first few sections of this chapter as you move through setup and start using your iPad. If you feel like you're getting overwhelmed, you may want to skip ahead to 1.6: Setting Up Your iPad, and then review the earlier sections when you're feeling a little more comfortable. In our experience, it's easiest to get the hang of using an iOS device by actually using one! Rest assured that your iPad is designed to be easy to use, and it will happily tolerate beginner's mistakes. Feel free to play and experiment – we promise you won't break anything. Now let's get your iPad out of the box and into your hands!

1.1 What's in the Box

Your iPad is ready to go right out of the box – no need to charge the battery or connect it to a computer. It really is as simple as turning it on and configuring some basic setup options. We'll walk you through the process in 1.6, but don't worry. This is about as simple as it gets.

When you open up your iPad box, you'll find the iPad itself in a plastic sleeve, as well as a USB cable, and a 10W USB power adaptor. Hang on to the power adaptor and the USB cable – you'll need these to charge your iPad, and while the current iPad model doesn't require a computer for activation, you may want to connect to one later through USB.

The USB cable connects to the iPad's power dock, located at the bottom of the device. The other end connects to your computer's USB port and to the port on the power adaptor. Go ahead and figure out how everything connects – it's not tricky, but it's good to familiarize yourself with the process. If you've used older iPads, you'll notice that the eight-pin "lightning dock" is a good deal smaller than the older thirty-pin version. It's also reversible, so you're guaranteed to get it plugged in right the first time!

You'll also find a white envelope with some of the most minimal documentation in existence – a card that labels the four buttons on the device, a product information guide with safety and legal notices, and a couple of Apple stickers. A word of warning: purchasing an Apple device has been known to lead to an excessive collection of Apple stickers.

1.2 The iPad Buttons

There are only four physical buttons on your iPad, but you'll want to locate them right away and learn their names.

Sleep/Wake (On/Off)

Hold your iPad oriented like a pad of paper. Turn it over. See the Apple design on the back? Be sure it's facing right side up, and then look at the top left corner. You'll see a circle (that's your camera) and a skinny little rectangular button. There's your sleep/wake switch, which also moonlights as your on/off switch. There are two ways to interact with this button. Press and hold it to power on your device (go ahead and do this, taking a moment to admire the gorgeous Retina display). Press it briefly without holding it down to put your iPad to sleep, and again to wake it up. To fully power off your iPad, press and hold the button until the "slide to power off" message appears. Swipe the circle with the power icon on it to the right to power the device off, or tap the circle labeled Cancel if you've changed your mind (see 1.4 to learn about tapping and swiping).

Volume

The volume control is located on the left side of the iPad, if you hold the device with the screen facing you. It works just like you'd expect – press the upper end to increase volume and the lower to decrease it.

Mute / Orientation Lock

There's a switch just above the volume control that serves as a mute switch by default. It can also be configured as an orientation lock, but we'll cover that later. For now, just know that you can set the switch so that the red dot is visible if you need to mute the device.

Home / Touch ID Sensor

This is a terrifically important button – it's centered at the bottom of the screen and has an outlined square icon. You can use this button to wake your iPad up, and you'll also use it to return your home screen (more on this in 2.1). On newer iPad models, including Air 2, Mini 4 and Pro, the Home button also serves as a Touch ID sensor. Touch ID reads your fingerprint, adding an additional layer of security to your iPad, as well as a boatload of convenience.

1.3 Other Hardware

Your iPad is equipped with all kinds of gadgetry, though you'd never know it to look at the sleek device. Here's an outline of your iPad's various ports and accessories.

Camera (Front and Back)

Your iPad Air 2, Mini 4 or Pro comes with a front-and rear-facing 1080p HD still and video camera (absent in the first generation iPad). It's tiny, but you can see the front camera just above the screen if you squint. The back camera's a little easier to find. It's just beneath the sleep/wake button. These will be two places you want to avoid with your fingers while shooting photos or video!

Headphone Jack

The headphone jack is in the top right corner, if you're holding the iPad with the screen facing you. It's a standard jack (3.5 mm), so expect most standard headphones and speaker cables to work.

Speaker

To find the speaker on iPad Air 2 or iPad Mini 4, turn your iPad over and look in the bottom left. See it? It's surprisingly good for its size. However, you may want to avoid muffling it while listening to music or watching video with sound. The iPad Pro has turned up the volume by including four speakers, which automatically adjust based on your iPad's orientation. In other words, iPad Pro sounds better and louder than iPad ever has before!

Dock Connector

The nine-pin port at the bottom is where your USB cable connects to the device. Note that this is not the same thirty-pin connector used on older iPhones, iPads and iPods, and may require new accessories for users who owned older Apple devices.

MicroSIM Tray

If you have a 3G/4G-enabled iPad, you'll find your SIM card tray on the left side of the device (with the screen facing you). You'll need a special tool to open it (or, alternatively, a paper clip and some patience). Wi-Fi only models do not include the tray.

Smart Connector

The Smart Connector is only found on iPad Pro. This connector, located on the side of the iPad Pro, looks like three circles. It allows your iPad to work with accessories, most notably the Smart Keyboard, without needing to pair over Bluetooth and without needing an additional power source.

A8/9 Chip and M8/9 Motion Coprocessor

You won't see Apple's blazingly fast A8X or its M8 motion coprocessor, but you have them to thank for the speed, power and functionality of your tablet. The A8X chip is a desktop-class processor that delivers amazing graphics quality, speed and more. The M8 coprocessor includes a gyroscope, barometer, accelerometer, GPS and compass that constantly record data that let your iPad know where it is and how fast it's moving at all times. The fact that the M8 chip is separate from the A8X processor means that you'll enjoy better performance and longer battery life!

The iPad Pro kicks things up a notch (well, okay, LOTS of notches!) with the A9 chip and M9 motion coprocessor. Apple claims that due to these innovations, iPad Pro packs nearly twice the performance power of the Air 2!

Multitouch Touchscreen

We've saved the best for last. You have no doubt noticed your beautiful 12.9-inch (Pro), 9.7-inch (Air 2), or 7.9-inch M(Mini) Retina touchscreen. It will respond when you touch it, rotate it, tilt it, or shake it, as you'll soon see.

1.4 Finding Your Way Around with Actions and Gestures

The iPad is designed to be as intuitive as possible, and there are very few skills you'll need to master in order to use it. The touchscreen is simple; a few basic movements will allow you to navigate your iPad smoothly and quickly. We've outlined the basic iPad actions in this section for your reference.

Tap

This is the "click" of the iPad world. A tap is just a brief touch. It doesn't have to be hard or last very long. You'll tap icons, hyperlinks, form choices, and more. Don't worry, it's not rocket science!

Tap and Hold

This simply means touching the screen and leaving your finger in contact with the glass. It's useful for bringing up context menus or other options in some apps.

Double Tap

This simply refers to two rapid taps, like double clicking with your finger. Double tapping will perform different functions in different apps. It will also zoom in on pictures or webpages.

Swipe

Swiping means putting your finger on the surface of your screen and dragging it to a certain point and then lifting your finger. You'll swipe to unlock or shut down your iPad using a slider graphic. You'll also swipe to scroll up and down and from side to side, or to turn pages in a reading app. Left and right and up and down swipes have added importance in iOS 9 – you'll use it to navigate through menu levels in your apps, through pages in Safari, and more. It'll become second nature overnight, we promise.

Drag

This is mechanically the same as swiping, but with a different purpose. You'll touch an object to select it, and then drag it to wherever it needs to go and release it. It's just like dragging and dropping with a mouse, but it skips the middleman.

Pinch

Take two fingers, place them on the iPad screen, and move them either toward each other or away from each other in a pinching or reverse pinching motion. Moving your fingers together will zoom in inside many apps, including web browsers and photo viewers; moving them apart will zoom out.

Rotate and Tilt

Many apps on iPad take advantage of rotating and tilting the device itself. For instance, in the paid app Star Walk, you can tilt the screen so that it's pointed at whatever section of the night sky you're interested in – Star Walk will reveal the constellations based on the direction the iPad is pointed.

In most (but not all) apps and in your home screen, rotating the iPad will cause the display to rotate in adjustment. This is great most of the time, but if you're reading a book in bed, it's possible to lock the orientation to prevent dizziness every time you shift position (see Part 2.5).

1.5 Typing on the iPad

iOS 9 introduced tremendous improvements to the iPad's native onscreen keyboard, including the new San Franciso font found on the Apple Watch and a much clearer system for knowing whether or not the keyboard is going to output capital letters. Best of all, the new shortcut bar and support for multi-touch editing gestures make it easier than ever to enter and edit text. If you have a Smart Keyboard or a third-party keyboard, you can also take advantage of vastly improved keyboard shortcut support.

To type on your iPad, touch any field or area of the screen where you'd expect to be able to enter text. This brings up the iPad keyboard. The first keyboard you see usually contains letters of the alphabet and some basic punctuation. iPad is smart – it will automatically capitalize the first letter of a sentence, and you can hit the space bar twice to insert a period.

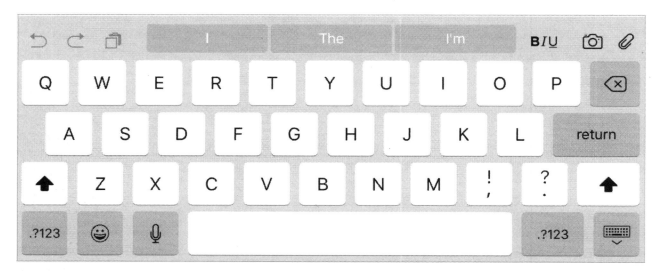

Screenshot 1: the iPad Keyboard

There are a few things to notice on the keyboard – the delete key is marked with a little x in the top right corner, and the shift key is the key with the outlined arrow, located on either side of the keyboard.

Using the Shift Key

To use the shift key, just tap it and then tap the letter you want to capitalize or the alternate punctuation you'd like to use. Alternatively, you can touch the shift key and drag your finger to the letter you want to capitalize (or the alternate punctuation). When you release your finger, the character is displayed. Try this out a few times to see which method is the best for you.

Double tap the shift key to enter caps lock (a typing mode in which every letter is capitalized) and tap once to exit caps lock.

Special Characters

To type special characters, just hold down the key of the associated letter until options pop up. Tap the character you want to use, and be on your way.

Using Dictation

If you're really struggling with typing, you can always turn on Dictation and give your fingers a rest. Just tap the microphone key next to the space bar and start talking. Dictation also supports punctuation. For example, at the end of the sentence you simply say "period." It also understands several other punctuation marks. It's not perfect, but you'll likely be surprised at its accuracy.

Number and Symbol Keyboards

Of course, there's more to life than letters and exclamation marks. If you need to use numbers, tap the .?123 key on either side of the space bar. This will bring up a different keyboard with numbers and punctuation.

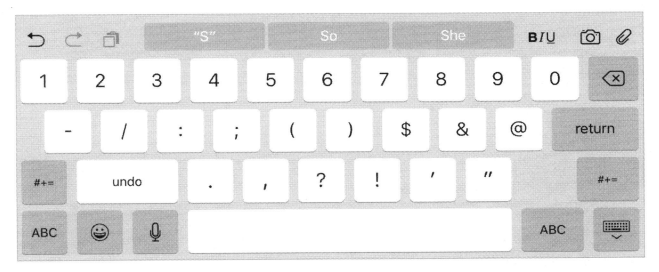

Screenshot 2: The Numerical Keyboard

From this keyboard, you can get back to the alphabet by tapping the ABC key on either side of the space bar. You can also access an additional keyboard which includes the remaining standard symbols by tapping the #+- key, just above the ABC key.

Screenshot 3: The Symbol Keyboard

To hide the keyboard, use the Hide Keyboard button in the very bottom right corner.

Emoji Keyboard

The emoji keyboard is accessible using the smiley face key between the 123 key and the dictation key. Emojis are tiny cartoon images that you can use to liven up your text messages or other written output. This goes far beyond the colon-based emoticons of yesteryear - there are enough emojis on your iPad to create an entire visual vocabulary. The iOS 9.1 update includes lots of essential new emojis, including a taco, a Vulcan salute, and a unicorn.

Screenshot 4: The Emoji Keyboard

To use the emoji keyboard, note that there are categories along the bottom (and that the ABC key on the far left will return you to the world of language). Within those categories, there are several screens of pictographs to choose from. Many of the human emojis include multicultural variations. Just press and hold them to reveal other options.

Screenshot 5: Multicultural Emojis

Configuring International Keyboards

If you find yourself typing in a different language fairly often, you may want to set up international keyboards. When international keyboards are enabled, you'll see a globe key between the ABC and microphone keys that allows you to switch between keyboards. To set up international keyboards, visit Settings > General > Keyboard > Keyboards (for more about Settings, check out Part 4). You can then add an appropriate international keyboard. iPad has great support for text entry in most major languages. For example, Chinese speakers can choose from pinyin, stroke, zhuyin, and handwriting, where you actually sketch out the character yourself.

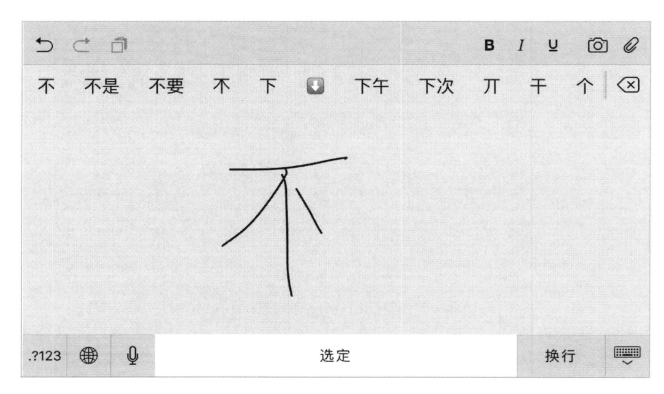

Screenshot 6: The Chinese Handwriting Input Keyboard

When you enable another keyboard, the emoji key will change to a globe icon. To use international keyboards, tap the Globe key to cycle through your keyboard choices.

QuickType: Autocorrect, Predictive Text and Shortcut Bar

Your iPad is loaded with features to help prevent slip-ups, including Apple's battle-tested autocorrect feature, which guards against common typos. The predictive text feature predicts what words you're most likely to type, based on your own past behavior. Three choices appear just above the keyboard – the entry as typed, plus two best guesses. Predictive text is somewhat context-specific, too. It learns your speech patterns as you email your boss or iMessage your best friend, and it will serve up appropriate suggestions based on whom you're messaging or emailing. You can turn it off by visiting Settings > General > Keyboards and turning off predictive text by sliding the green slider to the left (for more on Settings, check out Part 4).

Screenshot 7: Predictive Text and Shortcut Bar

On either side of the predictive text options, you'll find the shortcut bar. Here, you can use the arrows on the left to undo and redo edits. The clipboard icon allows you to paste copied content (more on this shortly). Over on the right, the **B/U** key gives you formatting options for bold, italicized and underlined text. You can also insert pictures using the camera icon or, in some apps like Mail, file attachment using the paperclip.

Selecting Text

To select text on an iPad, tap and hold over the text you want to manipulate. This brings up options to cut, copy, format, define, share, quote, insert media, or add attachments.

Screenshot 8: Selecting Text

It's much easier to select text in iOS 9, thanks to the two-finger multigesture that allows you to move the cursor. Just take two fingers and drag them over the screen to move the cursor. This makes it so much easier to position your selection over the correct word or to fix a typing mistake!

Third Party Keyboards

Like its predecessor iOS 8, iOS 9 allows third party keyboards. If you've been using the Swype keyboard on an Android device – rejoice! It's available in the App Store.

1.6 Setting Up Your New iPad

Setting up a new iPad is a breeze, thanks to iPad's built-in Setup Assistant. iPad will walk you through the initial setup step by step, and we'll give you the details as you go.

If you haven't done so already, press and hold the sleep/wake button to turn on your new iPad. Look at the bottom of the screen. You'll see an arrow and the message "slide to set up," which will cycle through several languages. Take your finger, touch the arrow, and swipe your finger across the screen.

Screenshot 9: The First iPad Setup Screen

Next, you'll be prompted to select your preferred language and your country or region. Select by tapping the appropriate text with your finger, and use the Back text in the upper left corner if you make a mistake or change your mind about anything while working through the setup process.

Now, connect your iPad to a wireless network, if one is available. You may need to enter a password. If you don't have a wireless connection, you can connect using cellular data if you have the 3G-enabled model, though remember that using a wireless network won't affect your data plan with your wireless carrier, while using 3G may count toward data plan limits.

Wait while your iPad is activated.

Now you'll decide whether or not to enable Location Services. Location Services add all kinds of fun and convenience to many apps – for example, Maps can find your current location and use it as a starting point for route directions, and Camera can automatically tag your photos with your location. However, this also means that you're allowing your device to read and transmit your physical location, and it can shorten your battery life considerably. You'll need to decide for yourself how you feel about this, though you'll be able to change your mind later.

Tip: the blue arrow icon displayed on the Location Services screen will show up in many location-based apps. Tapping it will usually reveal your current location on a map or information relevant to your current location.

Screenshot 10: Location Services

Next, you'll be prompted to set up your Touch ID. You can skip this if you want to, but we strongly recommend taking advantage of the security and convenience this feature offers. Touch ID will allow you to unlock your iPad by simply touching the Home button. You can also make purchases on iTunes or the App Store without entering your Apple ID. To set up your Touch ID, repeatedly touch the Home button until your iPad is able to read a complete print. This may take several tries, but don't worry – we've found it to be remarkably adept at reading your print after you complete this step!

Next, you'll also be prompted to enter a passcode. If you're using Touch ID, this will be required so that you can get into your iPad even if the Touch ID sensor malfunctions. Even if you've chosen not to use Touch ID, entering a passcode still isn't a bad idea. A passcode is a four-digit password that your iPad requires every time it wakes up. If that seems like a hassle, though, just tap Don't Add Passcode. You can always change this setting later if you need to.

After you've set up your passcode, decide whether or not to use Touch ID for the App Store and iTunes.

Screenshot 11: Creating a Passcode

Next, you'll have the option to restore from a backup. If you've backed up an older iPad either in iCloud or in iTunes, you can restore it here. Otherwise, just tap Set up as new iPad. Note that even if you do have a backed up version and want to start from scratch, it's fine to do so.

Next up is the Apple ID screen. If you already have one, go ahead and sign in. If you don't, take the time to create one now by tapping Create a Free Apple ID. Your Apple ID makes it possible to download apps from the App Store and content from iTunes. Without an Apple ID, you'll find it very difficult to get the most out of your iPad.

Screenshot 12: The Apple ID Screen

The Apple ID is completely free – just follow the prompts and enter the information requested. Be sure to choose a secure password that you can remember. You'll be using it every time you install a new app or buy a new song or video.

Now agree to the Terms and Conditions by tapping Agree, and then tapping Agree one more time in the box that pops up. It's a chore, but it's always a good idea to read through these binding legal agreements!

Wait a minute or two while your Apple ID is set up.

Now, decide whether you want to use iCloud Drive with your iPad. We strongly recommend opting in, especially if you have more than one Apple device. Of course, even if your iPad is your first foray into the Apple world, you could wind up with other devices or newer models in the future. iCloud Drive will make it much, much easier to transfer your purchased content and your photos, contacts, and other content to new devices later on, and it also opens up features like Find My iPad, which can be a lifesaver if your iPad goes missing. Find My iPad will allow you to locate a missing iPad, send messages to it, shut it down, password protect it, and wipe it clean remotely. This is a great security feature - if the unthinkable happens, you'll be ready (Location Services and iCloud must be enabled for this to work).

Next, decide whether or not to use iCloud Keychain. This is a password storage system that keeps your passwords synced between Apple devices. Using it requires an iCloud security code or another device with iCloud Keychain enabled.

The next screen asks you to confirm your iMessage and FaceTime settings. While your iPad isn't an iPhone, it comes surprisingly close in iOS 9!

Next, here comes Siri! Go ahead and select Turn On Siri for now. You can always turn him or her (depending on your preference) off later, but even if you're not sure it's necessary, you'll want the experience of conversing with this astute and occasionally witty digital assistant at least once. Trust us.

Screenshot 13: Siri

Finally, decide whether or not to report diagnostic and usage data to Apple. If you're worried about privacy, tap the About Diagnostics & Privacy to learn what information Apple will receive and how it will be used. We recommend taking this stuff seriously.

You have now arrived at the final screen of Setup Assistant, so get ready to start using your iPad! Tap Get Started to view your iPad's home screen.

1.7 iPad Pro Accessories: Smart Keyboard and Apple Pencil

If you are the lucky owner of a new iPad Pro, we strongly recommend considering two new accessories – the Smart Keyboard and the Apple Pencil. The Smart Keyboard transforms the iPad Pro into something much closer to a full PC. Unlike third party iPad keyboards, the Smart Keyboard doesn't require any switches, pairing, or even charging. It connects to your iPad and shares power with the device itself. The Apple Pencil gives you much more control, particularly in drawing and design apps, by letting you get to single-pixel levels of precision. It's even smart enough to register pressure, allowing you to manipulate line weight naturally. By tilting it, you can even add shading to your creations, just like using a regular pencil. The Smart Keyboard ($169) and Apple Pencil ($99) are sold separately.

To set up an iPad Pro Smart Keyboard, simply line up the keyboard with the magnetic Smart Connector on the edge of the iPad until you feel the iPad and keyboard click with each other. There's no setup, pairing or charging – it just works! The Smart Keyboard also folds into a stand and into a protective cover.

The Apple Pencil does require charging, and uses the same lightning cable that your iPad and iPhone use. However, it charges incredibly quickly – 15 seconds of charging should give you about half an hour of battery life. A full charge gives you about 12 hours of battery life. To pair a new Apple Pencil with your iPad Pro, just connect one end of a lightning cable to the Pencil and the other to your iPad.

Wrap Up

In the process of setting up your iPad, you've already learned and probably mastered some iPad basics, including tapping and swiping, and some of the more common navigational elements (arrows, sliders, dropdowns, etc.). So you already know a little more about what your iPad can do and how you'll get your iPad to do it. You've learned where to find all the buttons and hardware on the outside, and learned a little bit about how to navigate the iOS interface. You've also received a preview of some of the things your iPad's features – Location Services, Siri, iCloud, etc. So take a moment to congratulate yourself. You're well on your way to becoming an expert iPad user.

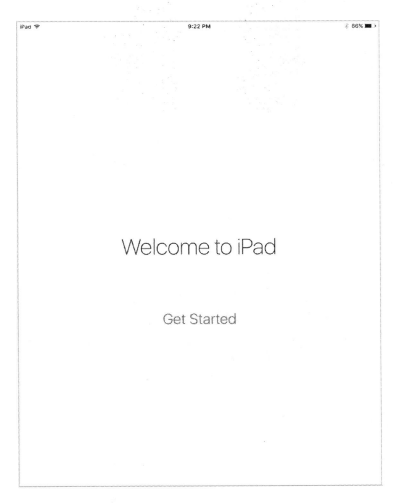

Screenshot 14: The iPad Welcome Screen

We're sure you're chomping at the bit to learn how to use the beautiful interface you're now looking at, so read on to find out exactly what your iPad can do!

Part 2: Getting To Know Your iPad

Your new iPad is all set up and ready to use, but where to start? This chapter will introduce you to the basics of the iOS 9 interface. In this chapter, we'll talk about using your home screen, working with apps, and finding other immediately accessible features.

2.1 Home Screen

We'll be referring to your home screen fairly often, and it's what you're looking at right now. The basic look and feel of the home screen hasn't changed much in iOS 9, so if you've used iOS 8 or iOS 7, you should feel right at home.

Screenshot 15: From left to right - iOS 6, iOS 7, iOS 8 and iOS 9

You'll return to your home screen again and again to launch apps, adjust settings, and check for updates. Microsoft Windows users may be looking for a start menu or a Documents folder. iOS is a very different operating environment, though. Everything you need is right in front of you... sort of. We'll help you dig a little deeper into your iPad's features in Parts 3 and 4.

2.2 Apps

"App" is short for "application." Applications are computer programs, like Microsoft Word, Photoshop, or Solitaire, to name some familiar desktop programs. Now, there are several apps that are included with your iPad (twenty-two, to be precise, plus your Settings area and the iTunes and App Stores), but the true power of iPad won't be fully evident until you start exploring the App Store (3.5). This is where you can find over one million apps for your iPad. Many are free and most are reasonably priced. If you can't wait to find out more, check out Part 6 for some recommendations.

For now, though, let's learn some of the basics of working with apps. You'll see all of your preinstalled apps on your home screen – the lovely little squares with rounded corners will soon become synonymous with work or play for you.

Opening and Closing Apps

Opening an app is as simple as touching it. Go ahead and open one of your choosing by tapping its icon. To leave the app and return to your home screen, press the Home button.

On the iPad, returning to your home screen is often all you have to do. However, it's simple to switch between two apps you're working with. Simply double tap the Home button to bring up the multitasking view. If you're done with an app, use your finger to "flick" it out of the lineup.

Screenshot 16: Multitasking View

This multitasking view is more than just an aesthetic feature – in fact, all iPad apps can run in the background and refresh themselves without being active. This is great news for a number of situations, but you may notice it has an adverse effect on your battery life. Fortunately, you can adjust your settings if you need to, and we'll show you how in Part 4.3. Apple has also worked pretty hard to mitigate the battery effects of background app refreshing. iOS 9 is smart – it knows which apps you use the most often, and it pays attention to network strength and time of day. As a result, your iPad will refresh certain apps more often than others.

SlideOver, Split View and Picture in Picture

One of the most exciting improvements in the iOS 9 upgrade is the ability to view more than one app at a time. There are three different ways to use two apps simultaneously on your iPad – SlideOver, Split View and Picture in Picture.

SlideOver is incredibly simple. To take a peak at another app without leaving the one you're currently using, slide your finger from the right edge of the screen toward the center. This will pull in the SlideOver column, giving you a sidebar view of available apps. Tapping an app will then open it in Split View, which divides your screen up equally between two apps. You can slide the divider between the two screens to adjust the space each app takes up.

Picture in Picture works with video-based apps like FaceTime. This feature allows you to minimize the video window so that you can use other apps without losing the video stream altogether. You'll find the Picture in Picture button in the bottom right corner of Videos. It's a box with an arrow pointing toward the lower right corner.

All native iPad apps support multitasking features, and many (but not all) third party apps do as well. Unfortunately, you'll need an iPad Air, iPad Mini 4 or an iPad Pro to use them – older iPads don't have the technical resources.

Badges

Screenshot 17: The Mail Icon with Badge

You'll be notified of new content or events inside your apps by badges – little red circles that appear in the upper right corners of app icons. The specific meaning of a badge varies from app to app – in Mail (Part 3.2), it means you have unread messages. In Facebook, it might mean you have new notifications, invitations, messages or friend requests. Generally, the first time you open them, apps will ask you to allow badges, alerts or notifications. These are called "Push Notifications." While these features can use up your battery pretty quickly, it's an easy way to tell at a glance whether or not there's something that needs checking inside your apps. Most of the time, you'll probably want to turn these on, but you can always adjust your settings later.

Organizing Your Apps, Deleting Apps, and Creating App Folders

You'll notice that four apps - Messages, Mail, Safari, and Music - are located at the bottom of the screen. This is a good place to keep the four apps you use the most often, because they'll always appear at the bottom of your home screen. You don't have to keep these four in such a prime location if you don't want to. Here's how to rearrange your apps.

Take your finger and touch one of your apps. Instead of tapping, hold your finger down for a few seconds. Notice how all of your apps start jiggling? When the apps are jiggling like that, you can touch them without opening them and drag them around your screen. Try it out! Just touch an app and drag your finger to move it. When you've found the perfect spot, lift your finger and the app drops into place. After you've downloaded more apps, you can also drag apps across home screens.

Screenshot 18: Apps in Jiggle Mode

Did we say home screens? Sure! Your iPad will display up to 11 home screens, and they'll automatically appear as you download apps. Just swipe to the right or to the left to move from home screen to home screen. Take a look at one of our home screens (pictured above), filled with apps we downloaded from the App Store. We're in the process of rearranging, so we've put all these apps in "jiggle mode." There's a difference here, though – see the little black X in the upper left corner of each third party app? By tapping that, we can delete apps that we don't want to use on our iPad anymore.

You won't be able to delete any of the apps that came preinstalled on your iPad, but you can at least put them out of sight and out of mind by moving them into folders. This is also a good way to increase the number of apps you can install on your eleven home screens, since each folder holds up to twenty apps (disc storage capacity permitting, of course). To create an App Folder, put your apps in "jiggle mode" by touching an app and holding your finger down. Now, drag one app on top of another. This will automatically create a folder. Go ahead and try this out – we can delete the result in a minute.

Screenshot 19: Creating an App Folder

When you create a folder, you'll be able to edit its name while in "jiggle mode." In the screenshot above, we've renamed a folder for the Game Center and Photo Booth. To delete the folder, just put all of your apps in "jiggle mode" and drag them out of the folder. iPad doesn't allow empty folders – when a folder is empty, iPad automatically deletes it.

Back

iOS 9 is full of small changes that have big impacts on usability and convenience, and the new Back button is one of them. Now when you're in an app, you'll see a tiny Back to [name of the last app you were in] link appear in the top left corner of the screen. For example, if you receive an email notification from Pinterest, you can view the notification in the Pinterest app and then quickly get back to Mail to continue working through your inbox.

2.3 Siri

You'll notice that there is no icon for Siri. If you've enabled Siri, press and hold the Home button. A microphone icon pops up, and Siri will politely ask you what it can help you with. Siri can help you with a lot, too – this feature is a massive feat of computer programming, capable of understanding natural language and delivering human readable/listenable results. Just tap the microphone to ask a question or make a request.

In iOS 9, you can also activate Siri without handling your iPad using the "Hey Siri" command. You'll need to enable this by visiting Settings > General > Siri. There, turn on the Allow "Hey Siri" toggle by sliding it to the right. From there, you'll be prompted to speak to your iPad so that it can calibrate your voice. Just follow the instructions until iPad tells you that "Hey Siri" is ready. Your iPad will need to be connected to a power source for this to work.

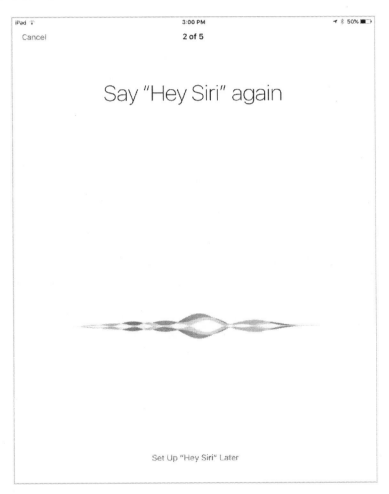

Screenshot 20: Setting Up Hey Siri

Siri is a powerful voice-activated system. You can ask her (or him) to adjust settings for you (e.g. "turn on Bluetooth"). She can also search Google, Twitter and Wikipedia for you. As in iOS 8, Siri can help you find sports scores, weather, and movie show times. He/she can also send text messages for you, initiate FaceTime calls, add Calendar entries, or give you directions. Siri also includes support for Shazam, meaning she can recognize songs for you. If you're not sure what's playing on the radio, just ask, "what song is this?" Siri will need to "listen" to the song to analyze it, and she will then give you an answer, along with either the option to buy the song from iTunes or listen to it in your Music app if you already own it.

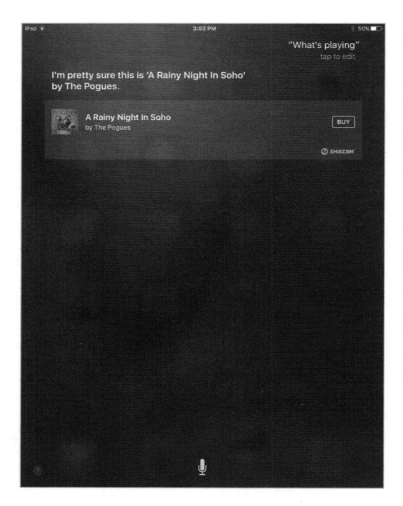

Screenshot 21: Using Siri to Find Out What's Playing

To get the hang of Siri, try some of the examples that pop up the first time you open the program. You can always access these later by tapping the little circled "?" in the lower left corner. Siri has added to her repertoire in iOS 9. Now you can ask extremely context-specific questions ("remind me to read this email later"), and Siri will work with you.

Screenshot 22: Siri Search Suggestions

2.4 Notifications and Widgets

Notifications can be configured in Settings, which we'll talk about in Part 4.2. For now, though, just know that notifications might include calendar events, new email messages, Facebook notifications, reminders, and Twitter notifications. You can access them at any time by swiping down from the top of the screen. To dismiss your notifications, swipe back up. You can access your Notifications Center from inside any app and even when the iPad is locked, though you can adjust these settings if you want.

As in iOS 8, if you receive a notification of receiving a new email, you can reply to it from the notification. This means that you can save time and effort by accepting calendar invites, responding to emails, returning text messages and more without ever having to open an app. You can also interact with notifications from your lock screen, unless of course you prefer to turn this feature off.

You can manage notifications interactivity on an app-by-app basis. Simply visit Settings > Notifications and find the app you need to adjust. You may want to do this if you're concerned about privacy, since your iPad won't need to be unlocked for someone to respond to messages.

Your notification center is streamlined into two categories – Today and Notifications. The Today tab includes today's weather, calendar entries, and more to help you organize your day. The Notifications tab includes every notification you've received. iOS 9 groups notifications by day, making them easier to manage and clear than the old app groupings in iOS 8.

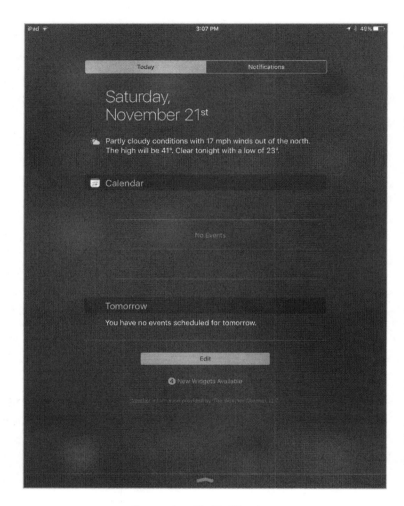

Screenshot 23: Notifications

The Notifications Center also allows you to install widgets. Widgets are tiny apps that run straight from the Notification Center. There's no need to open them or refresh them – they're just there when you need them. By default, your Notifications Today tab incudes the Weather and Calendar widgets, but we'll show you how to customize this in 4.2.

2.5 Control Center

Control Center is an easy way to get to the settings and apps you need the most often. Control Center is accessible by swiping up from the bottom of the screen. From here, you can put your iPad in Airplane Mode, control Wi-Fi and Bluetooth, set Do Not Disturb mode, and lock the screen's rotation. You can also adjust your screen brightness and access music controls. At the bottom, you'll see icons for the built-in timer and the camera.

Like Notifications, Control Center is accessible from inside apps and when your iPad is locked. You may want to disable this in Settings, depending on your situation.

Screenshot 24: Control Center

2.6 Searching Your iPad (Spotlight)

Searching your iPad for contacts, messages, apps and more is easier than ever in iOS 9, thanks to its new proactive assistant feature. The search function in iOS is called Spotlight, and it used to be reachable by swiping to the left on your home screen. Now, just touch anywhere on your home screen (besides app icons) and swipe down to activate Spotlight. This will bring up a search box where you can enter whatever you need to search for. Spotlight will search your music, email, contacts, calendar, podcasts, notes, reminders, messages and more – useful when your content lists start getting too big to scroll through! Spotlight takes search a step further by searching the internet, iTunes, and the App Store, as well as movie times, calculations, sports scores and nearby locations. It's a quick and convenient way to search without fumbling to open Safari or the App Store. In iOS 9, you'll also find a list of Siri's suggested apps at the top of the Spotlight screen.

Swiping right from your home screen will bring up a much more personalized screen that includes your most frequently accessed apps and contacts, as well as nearby locations and news items of interest. This content will change throughout the day, and as your iPad gets to know you, these suggestions will become even more accurately tailored to your habits and lifestyle.

Screenshot 25: Spotlight Search

In iOS 9, you can initiate FaceTime calls, Messages and more from the Search screen. Just tap on a contact to get in touch with him or her.

Tip: See the little magnifying glass in the search field at the top? Any time you see that in other apps on your iPad, it's usually a search button.

2.7 Using AirDrop

AirDrop was introduced in iOS 7, though Apple fans have likely used the Mac OS version on MacBooks and iMacs. In Mac OSX Yosemite, you'll finally be able to share between iOS and your Mac using AirDrop.

AirDrop is Apple's file sharing service, and it comes standard on iOS 9 devices. You can activate AirDrop from the Share icon anywhere in iOS 9. If other AirDrop users are nearby, you'll see anything they're sharing in AirDrop, and they can see anything you share.

AirDrop. Share instantly with people nearby. If they turn on AirDrop from Control Center on iOS or from Finder on the Mac, you'll see their names here. Just tap to share.

Screenshot 26: AirDrop

You can adjust AirDrop so that it shares with everyone or only with your contacts. It's a very easy way to move content from user to user.

2.8 Proactive Assistant

Proactive assistance is built into iOS 9. It refers to a collection of features that attempt to anticipate your needs by analyzing patterns in your behavior. It powers the new contact and app suggestions on the search page, and also helps guide your apps' behavior to minimize your need to enter information or tap through menus. For example, when you plug in your headphones, your iPad will suggest you start listening to the most recent playlist you were enjoying in the Music app. When you start a new Mail message, your iPad checks with you to see if you'd like to add contacts that you frequently use. You'll find these suggestions popping up all over iOS 9. It's one of the subtlest improvements of the software, as well as the most innovative.

Wrap Up

Now that you know how to use your home screen, open and close apps, and access Siri, Notifications, and the Control Center, you're ready to start learning more about the preinstalled apps on your iPad. But before you read further, take a few minutes and experiment. Talk to Siri, get your home screen arranged just the way you like it, and take a peek at some of your apps. You'll be using the information in this chapter over and over again, so it's a good idea to be sure you understand everything!

Part 3: Mastering Your Preinstalled Apps

In this section we're going to take a closer look at the apps that came preinstalled on your iPad. We'll give you plenty of help getting them set up and customized, but remember: these apps are only the beginning. If you're worried that they won't handle everything you want your iPad to do, remember that well over one million additional apps are waiting for you in the App Store!

We're going to approach the preinstalled apps in order, starting at the bottom left corner and moving to the right and upwards. Which brings us to our first and very important app...

3.1 Messages

This powerhouse of an app handles your text messaging, and then some! In Messages, you can send iMessages to any Apple-using friend or family member, without hurting anyone's carrier-imposed text message limits, and your messages can appear on iPhones, iPads, iPod Touches, or MacBooks running Mountain Lion OS or higher. In iOS 9, Messages can also send voice recordings and location information, as well as pictures and videos. You can start a group text conversation with the ability to name conversations, add and delete contacts within a conversation, and mute overactive conversation threads. Read on to learn how to get the most out of Messages for iPad!

Compose a Message

To write a new message, tap the NEW button in the top right corner. In the To: field, start typing the name of a contact, or enter a phone number if the person isn't saved in your contacts. Type your message in the text entry field and tap Send.

Once you've sent a message, it will display in Conversation View. If you need to see what time the message was sent, swipe to the right to reveal the time of each message.

Add a Picture or Video to a Message

If you'd like to add a photo or a video, tap the little camera button next to the text field. You'll have the option to take a photo or video or choose an existing one from your Photos app. Find the photo you'd like to use, tap Use, and when you're ready, tap Send to send the message.

Screenshot 27: Sending a Message with a Photo

In iOS 9 you can add more than one picture or video from your Photos at a time – this is a huge time saver for anyone who's used to adding photos one by one! To do this, select photos from the left-to-right scrolling view of your recent pictures that appears when you tap the camera icon. Otherwise, you can tap Photo Library to see your albums.

Send an Audio Recording

You can also add an audio recording to a message by tapping and holding the microphone next to the text message entry field. You'll then have the option to preview the recording, delete it, or send it using the upward-pointing arrow that appears in Recording Mode.

Screenshot 28: Sending an Audio Recording

Messages with Siri

You can also ask Siri to compose messages for you. Say, "Tell [Name of Friend] hi!" Siri will compose the message and ask if you want to send it. Say "Send" or "Cancel," and let Siri work his/her magic.

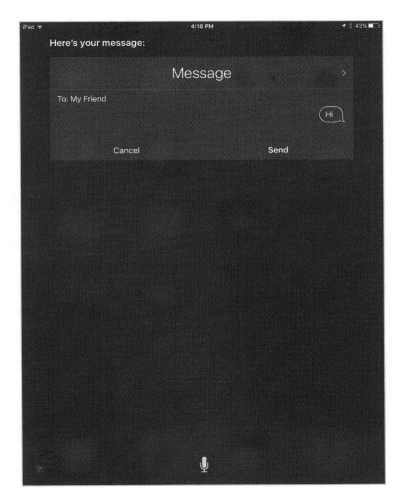

Screenshot 29: Sending a Message with Siri

Send Your Location

It's never been easier to answer the question "where are you?" than it is in iOS 9. To send a Maps snapshot of your current location to someone in Messages, tap Details in the top right corner of the New Message screen. Then tap Send My Current Location. This will send a picture of your location on a map.

You can also tap Share Your Location to allow your conversation partner to see your location for one hour, until the end of the day, or indefinitely – it's up to you.

Group Messages

Starting a group conversation is easy – simply enter multiple contacts in the To: field in the New Messages screen.

Once the conversation is going, though, you can add new contacts to the conversation without having to start a new thread. To do this, tap Details in the top right corner. There, you can add a contact by tapping Add Contact.

If you scroll down further on the Details screen, you'll also find the ability to leave the conversation entirely, or enable Do Not Disturb for that conversation, which will mute notifications. This is great for a large group text session happening while you're trying to finish dinner. At the very bottom, you'll also find every multimedia attachment from the conversation collected in one easy-to-use place – handy for extended family picture sharing!

3.2 Mail

Let's move on to our second app – iOS 9 Mail. If you're already using an email account, a calendar program, or a contacts manager, there's no need to reinvent the wheel on your iPad. Importing your accounts is easy, and only takes a few taps.

Importing Email Accounts

Tap the Mail icon in the bottom row of apps on your home screen. This will pull up a Welcome screen with a list of common mail services. Choose yours, and follow the prompts.

Screenshot 30: Setting Up a New Mail Account

If your email service includes calendars, contacts, notes, or similar features, you'll have the option to import them next. We strongly recommend importing everything you use regularly!

If you don't have an email address, you can create a free iCloud email account. Just go to either the Mail welcome screen or to Settings > Mail, Contacts and Calendars, and tap iCloud. An alert will pop up with the option to create an @icloud.com email address. It's free, so why not give it a shot?

If you have more than one email address, visit Settings > Mail, Contacts and Calendars to add additional accounts. We'll walk you through this process in 4.9.

Navigating Mail

Mail is simple to use. To check your email, open the Mail app. Mail will open to the last screen you viewed – the first time you open the app with a new account set up, you should see your inbox. Tap your inbox to see what's new. To read a message, just tap it. To return to your inbox, tap the text in the top left.

If you have folders set up, or you'd like to get to your sent mail or drafts, tap Mailboxes in the top left to get an overview of your mailboxes. From there, if you only have one email account synced in Mail, you should see your folders. If you have more than one account, tap on the account whose folders you'd like to view under Accounts. Then, just tap on the folder you'd like to look at.

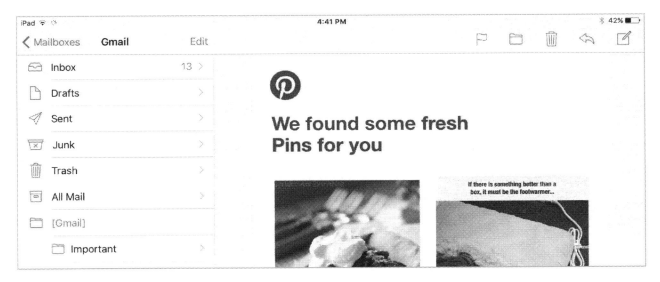

Screenshot 31: Viewing Mailboxes in Mail

iOS 9 also makes it easy to switch between your draft message and your inbox. To "minimize" a new message, swipe down to hide it and reveal your inbox. Just tap the New Message bar to return to your message when you're ready.

Sending Mail

To write a new email message, find the New button. Inside the Mail app, look in the top right corner for a square with a pencil in it. This is the iPad icon for NEW (you'll see it in Messages and other apps as well).

Tap it to start drafting an email. It's very easy to insert photos or videos from your Photos and Videos apps in Mail. Press and hold anywhere on the screen until the magnifying glass appears. You'll see some editing options. Use the arrow at the left to find the option to "insert photos or videos." If you tap this command, a box will pop up that will let you find and choose a photo or video. Find the picture you want and tap the Choose text in the bottom right. When you're done, just tap send!

Screenshot 33: Composing an Email with a Photo

Of course, you can also email photos and videos from the Photos app using the Share button. We'll show you how in 3.8.

iOS 9 Mail also includes the ability to add attachments from iCloud Drive or from third party storage systems like Dropbox. This is huge, since it allows you to mail files that may not correspond to an app on your iPad. If you have a Word document stored in iCloud Drive but don't have an Office 365 subscription, no problem. You'll find the option to add an attachment just after the option to insert a photo, as shown above.

Reading and Responding to Mail

Mail allows rich HTML messages, which means you can see images and photos in the body of the email without needing to download attachments. If you receive an attachment that needs to open in a different app, just tap the attachment and select the best application for viewing it.

In the Mail toolbar at the bottom of the Read Message screen, you'll see (from left to right) icons for flagging messages/marking them unread (the little flag icon gives these options when tapped), moving messages to a folder, archiving messages, responding to messages (with options for replying, forwarding and printing messages), and composing a new message.

Screenshot 34: The Mail Toolbar

In iOS 9, you can also swipe to the right to quickly mark a message as either read or unread.

Screenshot 35: Swiping Right to Mark Unread

Mail has gotten smarter in iOS 9. When you receive certain kinds of information in your inbox, Mail will give you suggestions, like adding addresses to contact names or adding calendar events for flight times or ticketed events.

Multiple Accounts

iPad makes it pretty simple to manage multiple email accounts. Inside the Mail app, you'll have the option to view all of your mailboxes. These include All Inboxes, VIP, your account inbox(es), and a list of linked accounts. You can get straight to your inboxes, or you can access any folders you may have set up by tapping the appropriate account. Take a look at the screenshot below to see what multiple accounts in Mail look like.

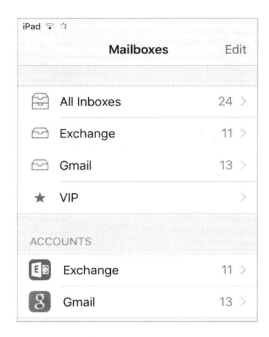

Screenshot 36: Multiple Mail Accounts

VIP

VIP is a handy feature for those of us who receive too much email. With the VIP feature, you can add your family, close friends, or boss to the VIP list and never miss an email you care about again. VIP emails will trigger banner and lock screen notifications, which are configurable in Settings > Notifications. This is a good way to be sure that you're alerted every time Mom emails you, but not every time that florist company you used once two years ago sends you a promotional email.

To add senders to your VIP list, tap the blue circled "i" next to VIP in the Mailboxes screen. Then tap Add VIP... to add new addresses. This will pull up a list of your contacts. You can also tap the Edit button in the top right to delete VIP contacts. Just tap the little red circle with a white line through it next to the offending name, and it's gone.

In iOS 9, you can also create VIP conversation threads. This is a handy way to keep up with an important conversation, even if you don't want to add every single person in it to your VIP list. To mark a message thread as a VIP thread, tap the Flag icon at the top right of the screen and then Tap Notify Me... Whenever a new message is received in the conversation, you'll receive an iPad notification (configurable in Settings).

Screenshot 37: Notify Me on an Email Thread

Deleting Messages

There are two ways to delete messages in Mail. You can delete a message after you've read it using the "Move to Folder" icon at the bottom. Just tap the icon and select your Trash folder. You can also bulk edit by looking at your inbox, tapping Edit, and deleting multiple messages by tapping the circle next to each message you'd like to delete and then using the Move button at the bottom of the screen to move them to your Trash folder.

You can also swipe to delete messages. Swipe toward the left to pull up the option to trash or archive a message (depending on your mail service), flag the message, or see more options, including reply, forward, mark as unread, move to junk, and move message. If you swipe further to the left, you'll delete the message in one fell swoop (swipe). We had a little bit of trouble with this – we found it very easy and convenient to swipe to delete, but had some difficulty stopping the motion in time to catch the More and Flag options.

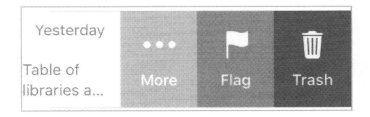

Screenshot 38: Swiping Left to Manage Mail

3.3 Safari

Safari is the iPad's native web browser (as well as the native web browser on Mac computers and other iOS devices), and it's better than ever in iOS 9. Safari is reasonably similar to Internet Explorer, Mozilla Firefox and Google Chrome, so first-time Safari users shouldn't feel too lost, but we'll cover the basics here to get you started.

Safari Basics

To get around in Safari, you'll most frequently use the search/address bar. Apple has unified the search and address bars so that you can type website URLs and search terms in the same place. This means that you can either type full web addresses, like www.google.com, http://www.minutehelpguides.com/, etc., or if you're not sure what the exact address is or if you're looking for websites about a topic, you can just enter keywords, like you would in a Google search. In iOS 9, Safari will suggest the top hit website for you, even if you don't enter a full URL. Try it out a few times to get the hang of using it.

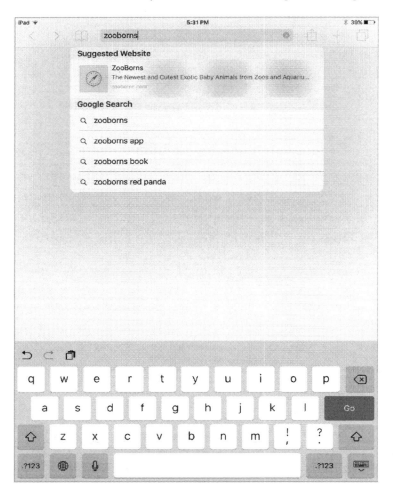

Screenshot 39: The Safari Search/Address Bar

As you scroll down to read a web page, the search bar will become inactive. This helps conserve screen space for reading, but just scroll upwards if you need to reactivate it.

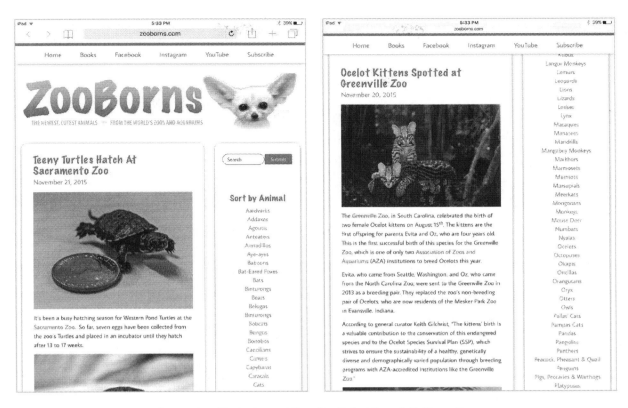

Screenshot 40: Active and Inactive Safari Search/Address Bar

Settings Tip: You can change the default search engine used by visiting Settings > Safari > Search Engine. Choose from Google, Bing, Yahoo! Baidu (a popular Chinese search engine), and DuckDuckGo.

Safari Tool Bar

The Safari Tool Bar is located at the top of the screen in the Safari app on either side of the search/address bar. It's only visible when the search bar is active, so swipe upwards if you can't see it. This toolbar includes six very useful icons. They are, from left to right, Back, Forward, Bookmarks (the open book icon), Share, New Tab, and Open Pages. Back and Forward (the two arrows) let you move back and forward through pages you've visited since you started browsing. The Share button lets you share the page you're currently visiting through Mail, Messages, Twitter, Facebook and more. We'll get your own social media accounts set up in 4.11. If you have clumsy fingers, these options will all bring up a popup box that will allow you to compose your share – if you accidentally tap a Share feature, don't worry, it isn't automatically pushed out without your approval! You'll also use the Share icon to bookmark a page, add it to your reading list or home screen, copy content, or print a page.

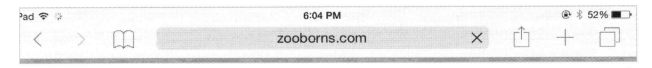

Screenshot 41: Safari Toolbar

The Bookmarks icon gives you access to your bookmarks, reading list, history, iCloud tabs, and more

(more on this soon).

Finally, iOS 9 for iPad gives you two different options for managing your open pages. The classic tab view is still there, and you can use the + sign at the top of the screen to add additional tabs. However, iOS 9 also includes the open pages card view that iPhone users know and love. To use this view, tap the two little squares at the far right of the toolbar. In this view, you can flick through your open pages and select the one you want just by tapping on it. You can also close pages by tapping the little x in the top left corner, and you can open a new page using the New Page button in the bottom center. You can also open a private tab by tapping Private. When you're done and want to get back to surfing, just tap Done in the bottom right corner.

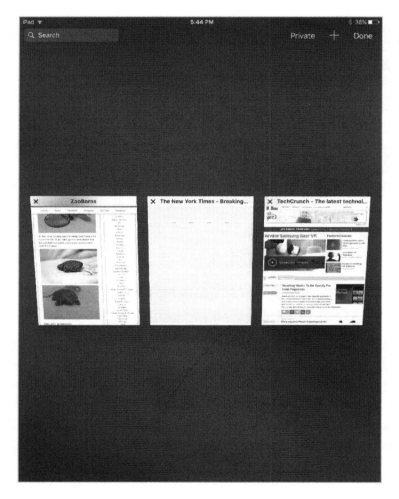

Screenshot 42: Safari Open Pages

If you've enabled iCloud tabs, you'll also see any pages that are open on your other iCloud-enabled devices listed at the bottom of the screen.

Safari Bookmarks

If you find yourself visiting the same websites over and over, think about bookmarking them to save time. A bookmark is a saved link to a web page that is added to a master list of saved links. You may already use bookmarks in other browsers; it's the same general idea in Safari. However, iCloud will sync your bookmark so that you can access it from all of your iOS devices, if you have more than one.

Adding Bookmarks

To add a bookmark in Safari for iPad, simply visit the page in Safari and tap the Share icon. Then tap Add Bookmark and edit your new bookmark. You can save it in an existing bookmarks folder by tapping location and then tapping your selection. Don't forget to tap Save to save the bookmark!

Screenshot 43: Safari Share Options

Using and Managing Bookmarks

To visit a bookmarked site, touch the Bookmarks icon (the open book icon in the Safari toolbar). To edit your bookmarks and/or put them in folders, touch Edit in the bottom right corner. You can delete bookmarks by tapping the red circle next to the name of the Bookmark you want to delete. You can also add a new folder by tapping New Folder in the bottom left corner.

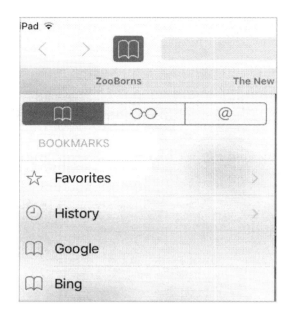

Screenshot 44: Safari Bookmarks

History

To access the history of webpages you've visited, tap on the Bookmarks icon. Then, tap History. History reveals every webpage you've visited since the last time you cleared your History, which you can do in Settings > Safari (see Part 4 for more about Settings).

Reading List

While reading an article in Safari, you can add it to your Reading List. Doing so allows you to come back and read articles at a later time. To add a webpage to your reading list, tap the Share button and then tap Add to Reading List. Like your bookmarks, your reading list is synced across all your iOS devices. Reading List actually saves entire webpages and stores them offline – this means that you can save lengthy articles for later reading, with or without Internet access. You can access your Reading List by tapping the Bookmarks icon, and then tapping the reading glasses icon, which represents your Reading List.

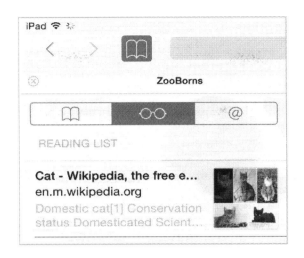

Screenshot 45: Safari Reading List

Shared Links and RSS Subscriptions

Safari also includes the ability to see what your Twitter friends are sharing, right from your bookmarks folder. Just tap Bookmarks, and then tap the @ tab to see what content is making the rounds in your Twitter feed. You will need to enable your Twitter account to take advantage of this, and we'll show you how in Part 4.11.

In iOS 9, you can also subscribe to RSS feeds through Shared Links. To do this, visit the site you'd like to subscribe to. Then tap the Bookmarks icon. Tap the @ sign, and then tap subscriptions in the bottom right corner. Tap Add Current Site to subscribe to the active site. This is very useful for blogs and other frequently updated sites you follow.

3.4 The iTunes Store, Music, Videos and Podcasts

We're going to talk about the Music, Videos, Podcasts and iTunes apps in the same section, since they're highly related. Music, Videos and Podcasts are essentially playback apps for content you purchase (or download for free) in the iTunes Store. To make iTunes Store purchases, you must have an Apple ID set up with associated credit card information.

Understanding Media on the iPad

The iPad is a powerful tool for playing video, music, podcasts, and other media. It's important to understand that you'll use the iTunes Store app for purchasing media and the suite of playback apps – Music, Videos and Podcasts – for enjoying that media.

Using iTunes

Launch the iTunes Store using the iTunes icon on your home screen. Look at the bottom of the screen for your main navigation – Music, Movies, TV Shows, Top Charts, Genius, and Purchased. In the Music, Movies, TV Shows and Audiobooks sections of iTunes, you'll see a category browser at the very top where you can browse by genre. If you know what you're looking for, use the search bar in the top right corner.

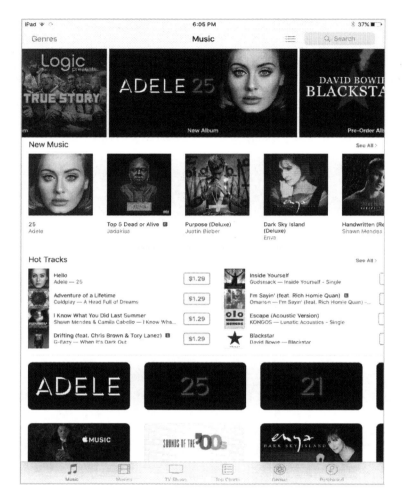

Screenshot 46: iTunes

Purchasing Content

When you find a song, show, movie or audiobook you'd like to buy, simply tap the button that displays the price. The button will turn green and display the message, "Buy Song." Tap the button one more time to make the purchase. You will be asked to enter your Apple ID or use your Touch ID at this point to complete the purchase. That's all there is to it – your content will download to the appropriate app (Music, Videos or Podcasts) for your enjoyment!

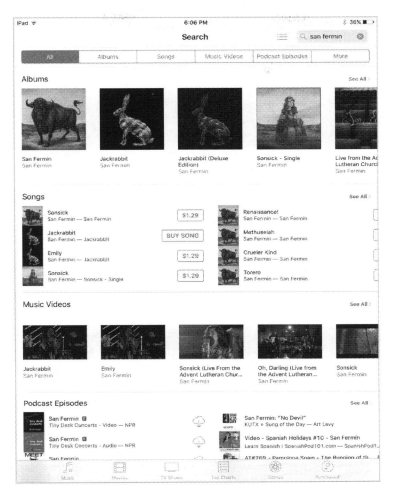

Screenshot 47: Buying a Song in iTunes

Note: Movies can be rented much more cheaply than they can be bought.

Genius

Genius makes calculated recommendations based on the media you've purchased. It's a nifty feature that can help you discover new stuff.

Wish List, Radio and Preview History
iPad will help you keep track of music you think you might be interested in through its wish list feature. iTunes will also keep track of each song or movie you preview and each song you listen to in iTunes Radio, which we'll cover shortly!

You can add items to your Wish List using the Share button. Radio, Siri and Previews will populate automatically based on your activity. You'll find all of these features using the menu icon in the top right corner.

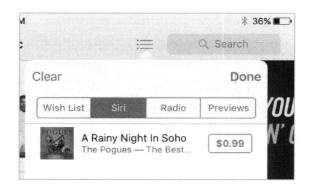

Screenshot 48: iTunes Wish List, Siri, Radio and Previews History

Purchased

If you've ever purchased music from iTunes, those purchases will show up in the Purchased section of iTunes on your iPad. Just tap the downward arrow in the iCloud icon to re-download them. How simple is that?

Screenshot 49: Downloading Previously Purchased Music

Music

The Music app, which underwent a fairly serious redesign in iOS 8.4 that carried over into iOS 9, features a streamlined interface for listening to your tunes. The main navigation at the bottom – For You, New, Radio, Connect, Playlists and My Music gives you several options for listening to and discovering music.

You'll find your own music in My Music and Playlists. At the top of the My Music screen, you'll find your music organized by artist, album, song, genre, composer, or compilation. The Playlists screen includes a mix of pre-installed "smart" playlists, like Top 25 Most Played, and your own mixes. In both the library and playlist screen, you'll find the ability to show only music that's available offline.

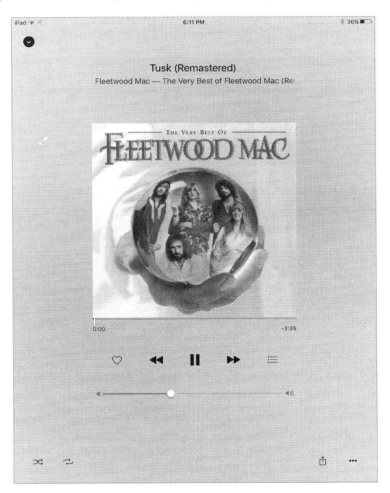

Screenshot 50: Music Playback

Music is very easy to use. While in the Playback Screen, you can set your repeating options by tapping the Repeat text in the top center of the screen. This gives you the options to repeat a song, repeat a playlist, or turn of repeating altogether. You can also create a Genius playlist based on the song you're listening to or an iTunes Radio station by tapping Create (read on for more information on iTunes Radio!). Shuffle randomizes your playlist order.

To return to your full Music library without ending playback, use the arrow in the top left corner of the screen. You can then return to the playback screen at any time by tapping Now Playing in the top right corner.

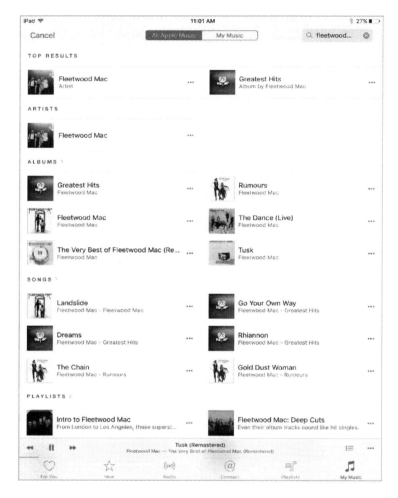

Screenshot 51: Music with Active Playback

Music will keep playing even if you leave the Music app or lock your screen. You can access Music controls within the app and from the Notifications Center.

Apple Music

Apple Music, which lives in the For You menu item at the bottom of the Music app, is a relatively new service from Apple that gives you the ability to stream the entire iTunes store and receive curated playlists from music experts tailored to your preferences. It costs $9.99 a month, but you can take advantage of the three-month free trial to see if this service is for you before paying for it.

iTunes Radio

iTunes Radio, introduced in iOS 7, is a streaming radio service based on your musical preferences. It's very similar to Pandora. To set up a new "station," just tap the plus sign labeled Add New Station (you may need to scroll down to find it). This brings up a list of genres. At the top, you can enter a song or artist you like, and iTunes Radio will build a station based on it.

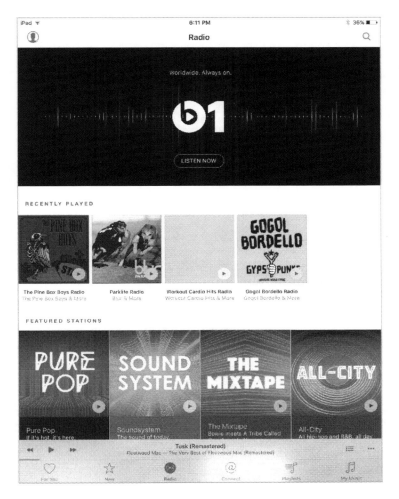

Screenshot 52: iTunes Radio

While you're listening to an iTunes Radio station, you'll have options to purchase songs as you hear them. You can also use the Star icon next to the pause button to let iTunes Radio know that you'd either like more similar songs or to never play a song again. You can also add songs to your iTunes Wish List from here.

Screenshot 53: Rating a Song in iTunes Radio

Connect

Music Connect allows you to follow artists (and actually it will automatically follow everyone in your library for you). It presents a Tumblr-esque feed of pictures, quotes and promotions from your favorite artists.

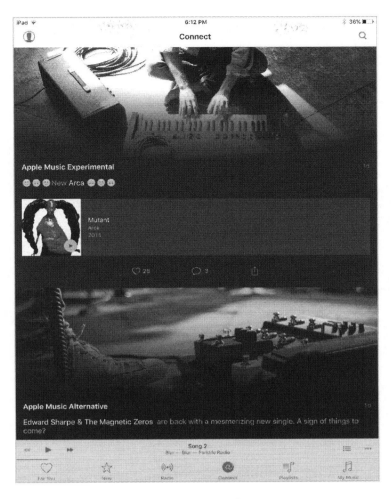

Screenshot 54: Music Connect

Videos

Any videos you purchase through iTunes, including movies and TV shows, will be played inside the Video app. Just like with the Music app, with the touch of your fingers, you can flick your way through your entire video library. Use the iPad smart cover to prop your iPad up for comfortable, hands-free viewing. Use AirPlay to stream to your Apple TV (the AirPlay icon automatically appears any time an Apple TV is detected on the same Wi-Fi network).

Screenshot 55: Videos

Note: If you use your iPad to shoot any videos yourself, you'll actually use the Photos app to view them. Confusing, we know.

Podcasts

There's a podcast out there for every interest and taste, and we can't imagine a long car trip without a fully loaded Podcasts library. There are also tons of free podcasts out there for your listening enjoyment.

Screenshot 56: Podcasts

In the Podcasts app, you'll see a menu at the bottom consisting of Unplayed, My Podcasts, Featured, Top Charts, and Search. Unplayed is a list of every unplayed episode, and it's a handy way to listen to everything you're behind on. My Podcasts contains every podcast you've subscribed to. Featured and Top Charts are good tools for discovering new podcasts to listen to, and of course Search allows you to find the specific podcast you're after.

You can choose to download your podcasts or to stream them. If you want to stream over 3G, you'll need to enable streaming in Settings > Podcasts > Use Cellular Data.

Syncing with iTunes on a Computer

While it's true that you don't have to connect your iPad to a computer to use it these days, you may very well want to. If you have a large collection of music files on your computer that were not purchased from the iTunes store, for example, you'll want a way to transfer them to your iPad. The good news is that wireless syncing is a beautiful reality these days. You'll need to connect your iPad with a USB cable once to set it up, and then you'll be able to sync over a wireless network happily ever after.

To set this up, you'll need the most recent version of iTunes installed on your computer. Be sure that your iPad and your computer are connected to the same wireless network. If both devices aren't using the same wireless network, you will not be able to sync wirelessly.

Connect your iPad using a USB cable. If iTunes doesn't start automatically, open it up. It should find your iPad, and you'll be asked to make some decisions about it. Follow the directions, and when your iTunes and iPad are talking to each other, find the option under the Summary tab that says "Sync with this iPad over Wi-Fi" in iTunes on your computer. Check it.

After you've successfully enabled wireless syncing, if iTunes is open on your computer, you should be able to go to Settings > General > iTunes Wi-Fi Sync on your iPad and tap Sync Now. Alternatively, you can rest easy knowing that the sync will happen every time you connect your iPad to a power source while iTunes is running on the computer.

iTunes Match

If you have an extremely large music collection, you may want to invest in iTunes Match. This $25 a year service analyzes your computer's iTunes music collection and then matches it with songs in the iTunes Store. If you've got iTunes Match, you can stream your entire music collection, including files that you ripped from CDs back in the dark ages, on all of your iOS devices, up to 25,000 songs (though songs purchased through iTunes don't count toward this total). We've found it to be $25 well spent – we love having all of our music on our iPad without having to sacrifice all of its storage space!

Once you've subscribed to iTunes Match from your computer, enable it on your iPad by going to Settings > Music > iTunes Match.

3.5 The App Store

To add new apps to your iPad, you will use the Apple App Store exclusively. Let's take a look around by tapping the App Store icon on your home screen.

Navigating the App Store is very similar to using the iTunes Store. The primary navigation links are at the bottom – Featured, Top Charts, Explore, Purchased and Updates. The Explore screen features regionally specific apps by top downloads and by category, as well as featured lists from Apple. When you tap the Search box in the top right corner, you'll also see trending searches – another handy browsing tool. There are also app category links at the very top. The Menu icon next to the Search box at the top will take you to your App Store Wish List, just as in iTunes.

Screenshot 57: The App Store

Other Official Apple Apps

The first time you open the App Store, you'll be asked if you'd like to download several official Apple apps, including the iLife suite (iMovie, GarageBand, iPhoto) and the iWork suite (Pages, Numbers, Keynote). These apps are free for devices purchased after September 4, 2014, and if you have a 64 or 128 GB iPad, they come preinstalled. Download any of these that look interesting!

Finding Apps

There are a few different ways to find an app in the App Store. If you know what you're looking for, enter the app's name in the search box in the top right corner. If you're in a more exploratory mood, take a look through the categories. First of all, go to Features at the bottom. Then, look at the top to find various categories (use the All Categories and More buttons to display more options). Apps are displayed in carousels. You can swipe across to see more, or tap See All for a list view.

If you want to see which apps are the most popular, check out Top Charts on the bottom. This helpfully displays paid and free apps separately – if you're on a budget, there's nothing wrong with perusing the free tab exclusively!

Purchasing and Downloading Apps

To buy an app, just tap the button labeled either GET (for free apps) or with the app's price. The button will then change to INSTALL or BUY. Tap it again. Enter your Apple ID or Touch ID when prompted. Then sit back as your app downloads. It really is as simple as that. You can watch your app's download progress with the completing pie chart graphic that begins with the download. You don't have to wait for the app to finish downloading before leaving the App Store or before opening a different app.

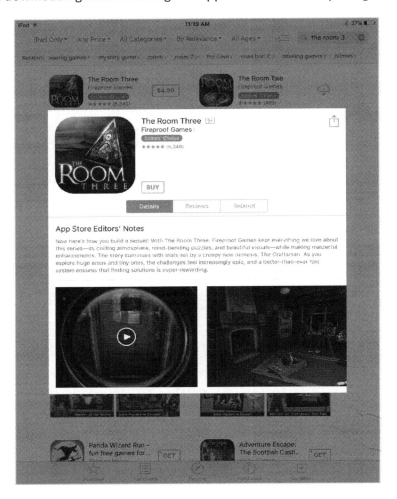

Screenshot 58: Purchasing an App

Downloading Free Apps Without a Credit Card

Free apps still require an Apple ID to download. If you want to download free apps, but don't want to set up credit card information with your Apple ID, this is your chance. Find a free app, touch the button that says FREE and then touch the button that says download. From here, follow the prompts to set up your Apple ID, and set the payment method to None.

Downloading Past Purchases

Tap Purchased at the bottom of the App Store screen to see a list of every app you've ever bought with your Apple ID. From here, you can re-download them if you need to.

Updating Apps

In iOS 9, apps will update in the background and the App Store will send you a notification when each update is complete. Of course, if you'd prefer to manage your updates manually, you can turn off automatic downloads in Settings > iTunes and App Store. Just switch off the Updates item under Automatic Downloads. This may be a good idea if you're concerned about buggy updates or losing features.

To manually manage your updates, open the App Store and tap Updates at the bottom. You'll see the option to Update All in the top right, or you can update apps individually.

3.6 FaceTime

FaceTime is Apple's famous video call service, and it's incredibly useful for families or friends who want to keep in touch with each other long distance. FaceTime is a video calling service, similar to Skype. It works over 3G or over Wi-Fi, meaning that if you have a limited data plan, you can still make unlimited FaceTime calls with a decent wireless connection.

Screenshot 59: FaceTime

Inside the FaceTime app, you'll find your FaceTime favorites, your recent FaceTime calls, and your Contacts. To initiate a FaceTime call, type a contact's name or enter an email or phone number. If you're camera-shy, you'll be glad to know that you have the option to switch to audio-only in FaceTime! Just tap on the telephone icon to initiate an audio-only call.

Screenshot 60: FaceTime Video and Audio Modes

3.7 Calendar

Calendar is an indispensable tool for keeping track of your busy life, and it's even smarter in iOS 9. Like Mail and Contacts, Calendar can be set up to sync with other accounts, like Gmail and Exchange. iCloud will also automatically import any existing calendars you've set up on other iCloud-enabled devices. If you need to sync another Calendar account, you can do so from Settings (see 4.9).

Screenshot 61: Calendar

Calendar can be viewed by day, week, month or year. Use the buttons at the top to switch view. You can also tap Today at the bottom to view everything happening today.

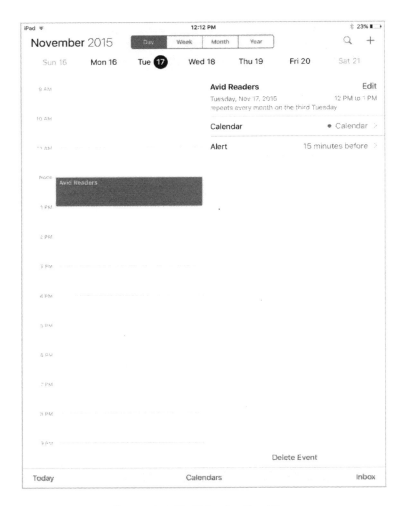

Screenshot 62: Calendar Day View

You'll also see Inbox in the lower right corner. This is where all of your calendar invitations will collect for your review and acceptance.

Adding Calendar Events

To add a new event to your calendar, tap the + in the top right corner. This brings up the Add Event screen. Here you can enter basic information about your calendar event. You can set repeating events, invite your contacts, set alert preferences, and add availability information, URLs and Notes. You'll see your calendar entries in your notifications, and if you set them to alert you, an alert message will pop up at the designated time.

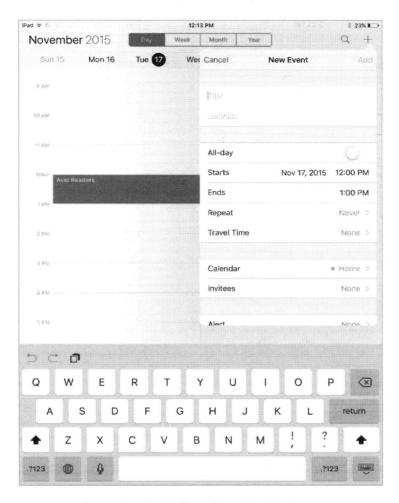

Screenshot 63: Adding a New Calendar Event

Calendar, like the rest of iOS 9, is smart. When you receive an email with important information, like a flight itinerary, Calendar will add that information as an event.

Managing Multiple Calendars

You can manage multiple calendars by tapping Calendars in the middle of the main Calendar display. This reveals every calendar currently connected to your account. If you want to hide a calendar without deleting it from your iPad, tap it to deselect it. Note that if you have enabled Family Sharing, a shared Family calendar will appear. This is a great way to keep track of everyone's dance recitals, conferences, and doctor's appointments. For more on Family Sharing, see 4.13.

3.8 Camera and Photos

The Camera and Photos apps on your iPad are a match made in heaven, especially with the powerful hardware of the newest iPad models. In addition to 8MP stills, the iPad Pro, iPad Air 2 and iPad Mini can shoot 1080p HD video. To help you organize and enjoy your photos and videos, the Photos app now includes much more intuitive organization and photo editing tools that make using it a joy rather than a headache-inducer. iPads have always been wonderful camera tools, but this generation is unparalleled!

Using the Camera

Taking a photo is as easy as point, click, and shoot, and capturing video is as easy as lights, iPad, action. To get started, open the Camera app. The camera app defaults to photo mode, but in iOS 9, just slide the mode text to switch to Time Lapse, Slo Mo, Video, Photo or Square to change modes. To take a photo, tap the large circle button in the right center. You can also turn HDR on and off at the top center. iOS 9 also includes a timer function, so it's possible to take a hands-free selfie. Just tap the timer and choose a 3 or 10 second delay. Finally, you can toggle between the front- and backward-facing cameras using the button in the top right.

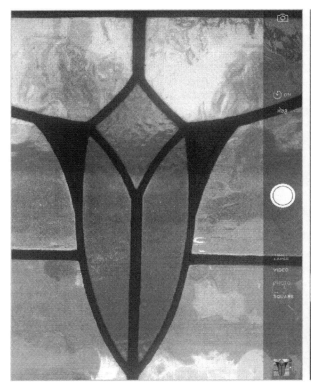

Screenshot 64: Photo and Video Mode in Camera

In iOS 9, you can adjust the focus and brightness of a picture before you take it. Tap on the area of the picture you want to focus on and then adjust the brightness scale that appears to your satisfaction. This is a huge improvement for serious iPad photographers!

Using Photos

The Photos app is your one-stop shop for organizing, editing and sharing your iPad photos and videos. Here you can browse and organize your photos, as well as share them with friends and family.

Navigating Photos

Photos includes three main screens – Photos, Shared, and Albums. To switch between these views, use the icons at the bottom of the Photos screen.

Screenshot 65: Photos Navigation

The Photos screen organizes all of your photos into Years, Collections (which are logical groupings of photos that iOS puts together for you) and Moments (a thumbnail view of all of your photos). Move from Moments to Collections and from Collections to Years by tapping the text in the top left corner. Move from Years to Collections and Collections to Moments by tapping the photo sets.

From Moments, tap on any photo to view it, edit it, share it or delete it.

Screenshot 66: Moments in Photos

In the Photos screen, you can also view your photos grouped by location by tapping on a place name in Moments, Collections, or Years. This will show a photo map view. Tap on a place to view all of the photos you took while you were there.

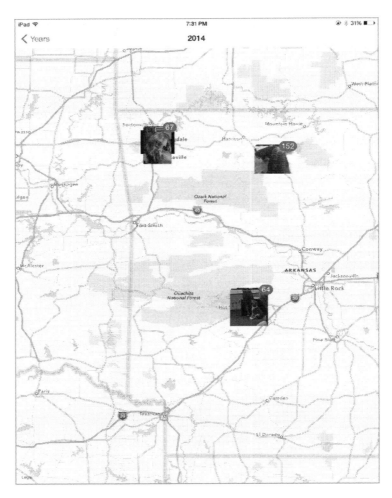

Screenshot 67: Photos Location Map

Shared Photos include any albums you've shared with others or that others have shared with you. It's very easy to set up a new shared album. Visit the Shared screen and then tap New Shared Album. Give the album a name and then select people to share it with. Next, select pictures to share. You can add pictures to this album at any time and they'll automatically appear in your selected contacts' Photos app. View all of the activity in your shared photos by tapping Activity at the top left of the Shared screen.

Finally, the Albums screen displays any albums you've created, as well as some iOS 9 default albums, which are exactly what they sound like – All Photos, Recently Added, Favorites, Videos, Slo-mo, Time-lapse, and Recently Deleted (note that these may not appear until you've taken the right kind of photo or video). There are two notable album additions in iOS 9 – Selfies and Screenshots! Photos will automatically add pictures taken with the front-facing camera to the Selfies album, making it easy to find your best selfie shots. Similarly, any screenshots you take (hint: hold down the Home button and the power button at the same time to take a screenshot) will be saved in the Screenshots album.

When you're looking at a photo, you'll also find a scrolling scrubber photo track underneath it (new to iOS 9), making it much easier to navigate a set of photos than the old method of switching back to the album view.

My Photo Stream

My Photo Stream stores up to 1000 photos in the cloud for you and delivers them to every iCloud- and My Photo Stream-enabled device that's associated with your Apple ID. The catch, of course, is that it will ONLY store 1000 photos, and it will only store photos from the last 30 days. After you reach 1000 photos or the 30-day limit, whichever happens first, the oldest photos will be removed from My Photo Stream to make room for newer ones.

My Photo Stream is a great way to get quick access to your most recent photos, without needing to mess with iCloud Photo Library or pay for extra storage. iCloud includes 5 GB of free storage, but My Photo Stream does not count against that limit. You can enable it in Settings > iCloud > Photos.

iCloud Photo Library

iCloud Photo Library is a service that allows you to save all of your photos stored in the Photos app (either on a Mac or on an iOS device). The catch there is that most of us have photo libraries that exceed the 5 GB of free storage Apple allows. Fortunately, if you have a large library that you'd like to back up using iCloud, extra storage is fairly cheap.

Creating and Managing Photo Albums

To create a new album, tap the + in the top left corner of the Albums screen. Give your new album a name and then select the photos you want to include by tapping them. Tap Select and then Done to save the photos to the album.

Screenshot 68: Selecting Photos for an Album

To add photos to an existing album, tap Select in the top right corner of the screen. Select the photos you'd like to add by tapping them and then tap Add To. Tap the appropriate album to finish the process. You can also create a new album by using Select and Add To – instead of choosing an existing album, scroll all the way to the bottom and tap New Album.

To manage your custom albums, tap Edit in the top right corner of the main Albums screen. To delete a custom album, tap the red circle that appears next to it. This will delete the album, but not the photos themselves. To move it, use the three lines that appear to the right of the album name to drag it up or down. To rename the album, tap its name to bring up the keyboard. You can only edit and delete custom albums.

Editing Photos

iOS 9 allows users to make a fairly broad selection of edits to an image directly in the Photos app. To access them, open a photo and tap Edit. At the bottom of the Edit screen, you'll see options to auto-enhance, crop, add a filter, and adjust the brightness, color or saturation. After you've made your changes, tap Done if you're satisfied with your edits, and Cancel if you're not.

Screenshot 69: Editing a Photo and Applying a Filter

Sharing Photos

Photos can be shared individually by using the Share button in the bottom right when viewing a single photo. Photos can be shared through Messages, Mail, iCloud Photo Sharing, Twitter, Facebook, or Flickr, or you can assign photos to contacts, print them, copy them, or set them as your iPad's wallpaper. Swipe right and left to see all of the sharing options available to you.

Screenshot 70: Sharing Photos

Searching and Favoriting Photos

iOS 9 introduces a few other useful tools for finding photos. Use the heart in the top right of the screen to add a photo to the built-in Favorites album. Use the magnifying glass at the top of the Photos screen to search for places and dates. You can also use search suggestions as a fun, guided way to find the perfect Throwback Thursday post. In iOS 9, Siri can also help you search your photos. For example, you can say, "Show me photos from Florida last May," and Siri will pull up exactly what you're looking for.

Hiding Photos

In iOS 9, you can hide photos that you don't want to display. To do this, select the photo using the Select command in the top right corner of a photo display screen. Then tap the Share icon (counterintuitive, we know). Tap Hide and the photo will disappear. Hiding a photo will remove it from Moments, Collections and Years, but it will still appear in Albums.

3.9 Contacts

Contacts are wonderful, especially when they sync this reliably and painlessly. Contacts can also be synced with outside contact lists (from Exchange or Gmail, for example). iCloud will help you keep all your contacts in sync between all of your iCloud-enabled devices. If you didn't already import contacts when you set up your mail account, you can do it the first time you open the Contacts app.

Contacts can integrate with Facebook and Twitter, as well as iCloud and a number of other contacts managers you may be using (Gmail, Exchange, etc.). While the Contacts app is a wonderful reference tool, you'll find you use it the most inside other apps, like Mail, FaceTime, and Messages.

Adding Contacts

To manually add a new contact, click the little + sign at the top of the Contacts display, then enter the name and information of the contact. You can assign ring tones for FaceTime and text tones for Messages on an individual basis if you like. You can also assign a photo to a contact by tapping the Add Photo box. This will give you the option to take a photo or choose one from your Camera Roll, Photo Stream, or other photo albums you may have set up (3.8).

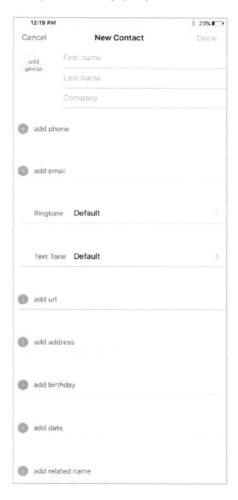

Screenshot 71: Adding a New Contact

If you have several numbers for the contact you'd like to add, additional phone number fields will appear after you start typing in the "mobile" field. You can also change the "mobile" label by tapping it. Similarly, you can add multiple email addresses and physical addresses. You can also add notes to your contacts, or several additional fields (Job Title, Birthday, etc.) as needed. You'll need to scroll down a little bit to access all of your Contacts options.

You can also edit existing contacts by finding them in your contact list, tapping their name, and tapping Edit in the top right corner. iCloud will sync your contacts across your devices, so if you add a contact on your iPad, it will automatically appear on your iCloud-enabled iPhone or Mac.

Using Contacts

You'll use your iPad Contacts list all the time – from each Contacts entry, you can choose to send a message, make a FaceTime call, share the contact, or add the contact to your Favorites list. Of course, you can also do these things through the respective apps. Just start typing a contact's name in Messages, FaceTime, etc., and the app will access Contacts for you.

3.10 Clock

The iPad clock app is extremely handy – it includes a customizable world clock, an alarm, a stopwatch and a timer, all of which work beautifully.

World Clock

The world clock allows you to create a list of locations and view the current time at a glance. This is particularly useful for anyone with friends, family or business partners in different time zones. To add places to the World Clock list, just tap the circled +.

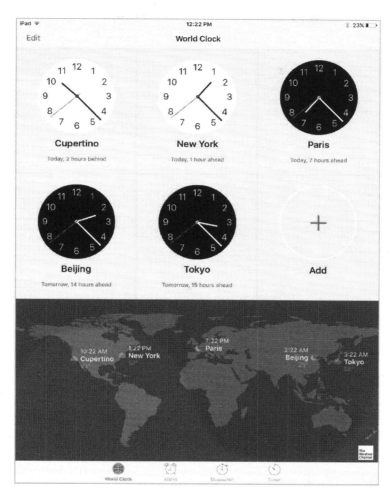

Screenshot 72: World Clock

Alarm

Alarms can be set by tapping Alarm at the bottom of the screen, and then tapping the + button in the top right corner. This brings up the Add Alarm box. Adjust the time by swiping up and down the dials for hours and minutes (and don't forget about AM and PM!). You can also set the alarm to repeat every Monday, Tuesday, Wednesday, etc.

Screenshot 73: Alarm

If you've had about enough of the default alarm tone, you can choose a different sound. You can also use Pick a Song to access your iTunes library or purchase ring tones from iTunes.

To delete alarms, use the Edit button in the top left corner. This brings up a list of every saved alarm. Tap the red circle next to the alarm you want to delete to bring up the delete button, and then tap Delete.

When your alarm sounds in the morning, unlock your iPad to turn it off, or tap Tap to Snooze for a few more precious minutes.

Stopwatch

The iPad Stopwatch consists of an elapsed time display, a Start button, and a Reset button. Tap Start to start the clock, and then use Lap to record a lap, and Stop to stop the clock. Laps are recorded underneath the elapsed time.

Screenshot 74: Stopwatch

Timer

The Timer feature lets you set the length of time you want to count down, and gives you buttons for starting and pausing the timer. Use the Sounds button in the top right to change the sound the timer makes when it hits zero.

Screenshot 75: Timer

3.11 Maps

Maps is Apple's in-house answer to Google Maps (though of course, if you're a Google Maps devotee, you can always download the Google Maps app from the App Store). It makes use of Location Services to serve up relevant information based on your current location and includes a number of handy features like directions, satellite view, Yelp review integration, and more. iOS 9 adds the ability to navigate public transportation in several major cities, meaning it's never been easier to find your way around a new city.

3D and Satellite View

If Location Services are enabled, Maps will reveal your current location with a blue dot when you tap the location arrow in the bottom left corner. You can also view the map area in 3D, if you're in a supported location, by tapping 3D. For more options, tap the circled "i" icon at the bottom right. Here, you can change the view to a satellite or hybrid view, print, show traffic, or drop pins.

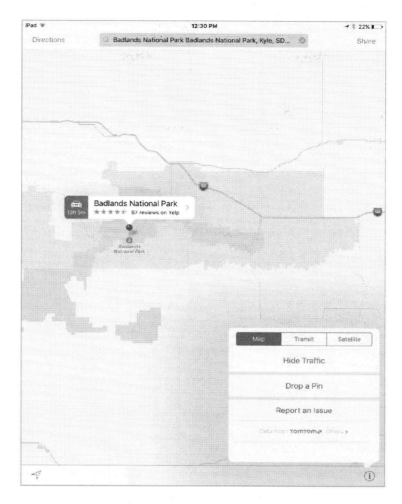

Screenshot 76: Maps Options

Places and Favorites

iPad Maps allows you to mark locations for later reference and learn more about them. Any time you see a place name, just tap it to find out more about the place. You'll also have options to save the address in your Contacts, share the location, or add it to your Maps bookmarks (bookmarks in Maps are saved locations that you can access when you either search or get directions). Scroll down to see all the place options.

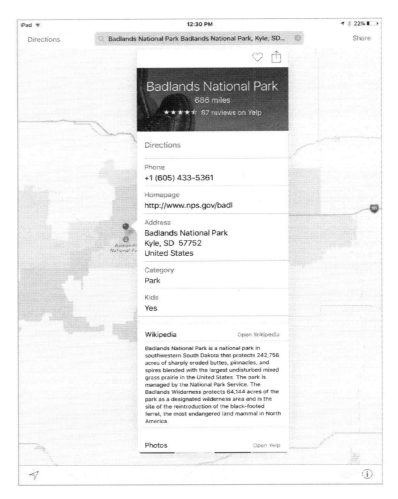

Screenshot 77: Place Information in Maps

Directions

To get turn-by-turn directions, touch the Directions icon in the top left corner. Enter your start and end locations. If you need to start from your current location, type "Current Location," if it's not already filled in. Then click Route to preview your trip and to choose an alternate route if you desire (to select alternate routes, simply tap them on the map). Notice that you can choose between walking, driving and public transit route options in iOS 9. If Transit view is available, it will also include schedules and other relevant information to help you accurately estimate how long your trip will take.

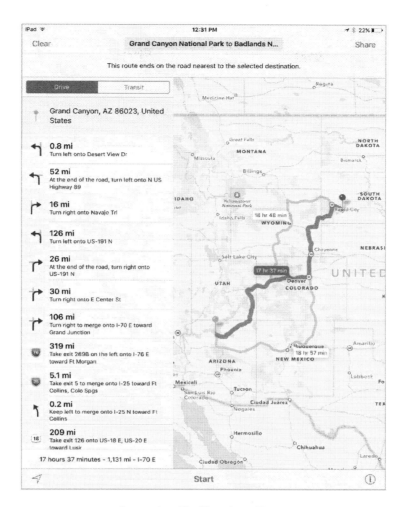

Screenshot 78: Choosing a Route

Click Start to start your trip! iOS 9 uses guided voice navigation so you never need to worry about missing your turn. You can always look over the full direction set by tapping Overview in the top right corner. To end guided navigation, tap End in the top left corner.

Nearby

Nearby is a new feature in iOS 9 Maps designed to help you explore an unfamiliar area. To use it, enter an address or use your current location. Then tap on the address bar. This will pull up the Nearby menu, which includes food, drinks, shopping, travel, services, fun, health and transport. You'll find subcategories in each main category. It's a great way to find the nearest coffee shop or shoe store.

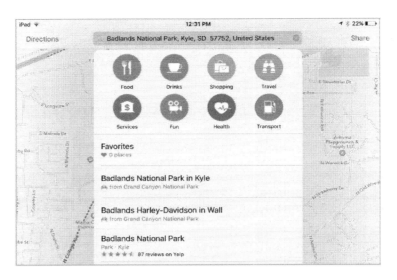

Screenshot 79: Nearby in Maps

3.12 Notes

Notes has been an unobtrusive feature of iOS from the beginning. It's always been a handy scratch pad for jotting down quick thoughts and stray observations. However, in iOS 9, Notes has evolved from a handy utility into a full-featured productivity app that rivals the likes of Evernote and Wunderlist.

At first glance, there isn't much to Notes. At the top of the Notes screen, you have some very basic options, including a Share button, a Trash icon, and a New icon. Tap the New symbol to create a note, which will be synced across all of your iCloud-enabled devices.

Screenshot 80: Notes

In iOS 9, you'll find an additional menu in Notes just above the keyboard. Tap the + sign to reveal it. Here, you'll be able to add checklists, images and sketches, vastly extending Notes' usefulness.

Screenshot 81: Checklists and Sketches in Notes

You can also use Notes without typing by asking Siri. Tell her, "Note that I'm ready to start using Notes!" and watch what happens. Siri will add a new Note that you can read by opening the Notes app and tapping the Notes button in the top left corner. With iCloud, any notes you create will automatically sync across all enabled devices.

iOS 9 also adds Notes to the Share menu, meaning you can easily store pictures, maps, links and other content in Notes, helping you keep track of all of your ideas, inspiration, sources, etc. in one iCloud-enabled spot. Anything besides plain text is added as an attachment to a note. The Notes app also gives you an Attachments browser (the four small squares in the lower left corner of the main Notes screen), where you can see every attachment in your Notes app. This is extremely useful when you start losing track of which note includes what information.

3.13 Reminders

If you're an obsessive to-do list kind of person, then Reminders is the app for you. It can import Tasks from Outlook or other similar programs, and you can create custom To-Do lists. Your iPad will remind you through sounds, notifications, and badges that you've got things to do. Check off list items as you accomplish them.

Adding Reminders

To add a new reminder, just tap a line in the Reminders app and start typing. Enter a title for the reminder. If you want to add additional information, tap the little blue "i" next to the reminder. This will bring up a Details screen where you can ask your iPad to remind you on a certain day at a certain time. You can also set a repeat reminder that will activate every day, week, two weeks, month and year by tapping Repeat. You can also prioritize your list so that the most important things get taken care of first.

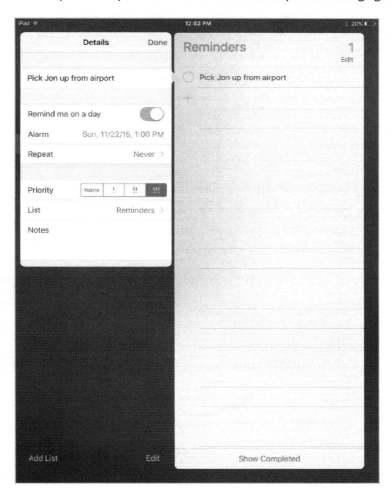

Screenshot 82: Reminder Details

Managing Reminders

To delete reminders, tap Edit and then tap the red circle next to each reminder you want to delete. To mark a reminder complete (without deleting it), just tap the little circle next to it. You can also tap Completed in the left menu to view reminders you've already dealt with. You can organize your reminders into lists by tapping Add List at the bottom.

iCloud will sync your reminders across all your iCloud-enabled devices. A word of warning: this can result in a lot of noise if you're in the same room with your iPad, iPhone, and Mac when a group of reminders starts buzzing!

If you've enabled Family Sharing, you can also make use of a special shared reminder list called Family. This list will be synced across all family members' devices. For more information on Family Sharing, check out Part 4.13.

3.14 Photo Booth

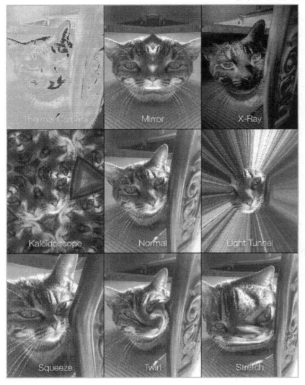

Screenshot 83: Photo Booth

With its dual-facing camera, your iPad just became your own private photo booth. To get started, tap the Photo Booth app.

You'll see an image of yourself or whatever you're pointing the camera at displayed in real-time in the photo booth window. To take a standard picture, press the camera button at the bottom center of the screen. To switch between the front and back facing cameras, tap the spinning camera icon in the lower right corner. If you want to have a little fun with your photo, add an effect. You can chose from a wide variety photo effects that squeeze, twirl and stretch your image. Your photos are saved to the camera roll in the Photos app (Part 3.8).

3.15 Game Center

Game Center is Apple's social gaming network. It lets you connect and play with friends (old and new) online, compete for top spots on leaderboards, and earn public points and achievements. If you have plans to play any social games on your iPad, it's a good idea to set up a Game Center account. If you change or add iOS devices, you'll be able to keep your game contacts in the process.

Not every game available in the App Store is Game Center-enabled, though a large number are, including many of the most popular (Angry Birds, Plants versus Zombies, Clash of Clans, et al.). You can search Game Center games from within the Game Center app.

Once you sign in to Game Center, you'll be signed in permanently (unless you manually sign out). If you choose to opt out of Game Center and instead walk the path of the solitary Fruit Ninja, Game Center will pester you every time you open a Game Center game, reminding you that you're not signed in.

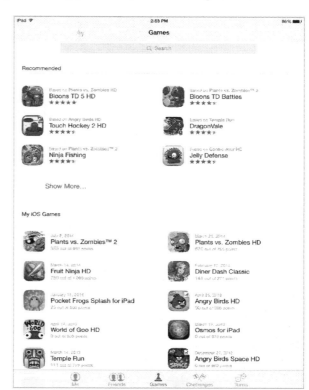

Screenshot 84: Game Center

3.16 News

News is brand new in iOS 9, and replaces the old Newsstand app. Rather than the app collection approach that Newsstand took to presenting periodicals on the iPad, News embraces a magazine-style presentation that's similar to the popular Flipboard app. It's a perfect interface for consuming articles from your favorite news sources and magazines.

When you first open News, you'll be asked to choose some sources to get you started. Choose from standards like CNN, Wired, Vox, etc. This will build a customized news feed for you that you'll find in the For You tab in the News app.

Screenshot 85: News for You

You can also explore topics and "channels" using the Explore tab, or search for information using Search. The topics list is enormous and includes just about any interest you might have. Adding favorites and reading stories will help News get to know your interests and preferences, and you'll find that your feed gets better and better the more that you use it.

When you're reading a story in News, you'll find options to share, favorite or save the story at the top of the screen. Favoriting stories that you really enjoy will help News deliver the most relevant content to you. If you've found a long form article that looks interesting but you don't have time in the grocery store line to read the whole thing, just tap the bookmark icon. This will move the story to the Saved tab on the main screen so you can read it at your leisure.

3.17 iBooks

iBooks is Apple's answer to Amazon's Kindle platform. iBooks opens with the My Books bookshelves displayed. As in other Apple storefront apps, a toolbar at the bottom helps you navigate between your purchased books, featured items, top charts, Apple Store search, and Purchased Items. These functions work just like they do in iTunes and the App Store. Note that in iOS 9, Apple Audiobooks can be purchased and enjoyed through the iBooks app instead of iTunes/Music.

Screenshot 86: iBooks

Reading books in iBooks is similar to most other e-reading apps. Tap the right and left sides of the screen to turn pages, and tap in the center of the screen to display menu options. While inside an iBook, the menu icon will take you to the table of contents, the text icon allows you to resize the font for your reading comfort, the magnifying glass searches the whole book for words or phrases, and the bookmark icon allows you to bookmark specific pages for later. Your bookmarks are accessible using the menu icon at the top. At the bottom of the screen you'll see a progress bar and the number of pages left in each chapter.

3.18 Tips

Tips offers bite-sized bits of advice for using your new iPad and iOS 9. At the time of writing, there are fourteen tips available (and they're all covered in this guide), but expect Apple to update this regularly.

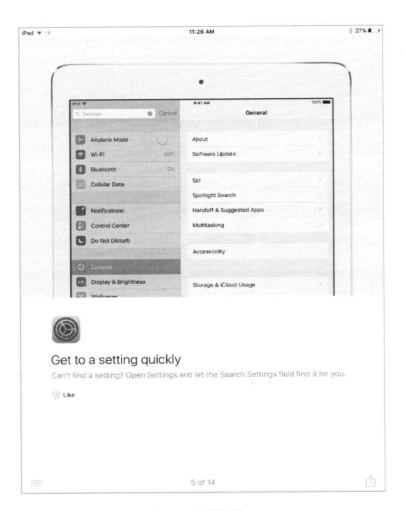

Screenshot 87: Tips

3.19 Find My Friends

Find My Friends is a social people finder app that can also be run as a widget in your Notifications center. The app displays a map that shows exactly where your friends are and how far away they are from you. You'll have to add friends using the Add function in the top right corner, and your friends will have to approve the service. You can even set up notifications that alert you when a friend leaves or arrives at a specified location by tapping a friend's icon in the app and then tapping Notify Me.

3.20 Find iPhone

Find iPhone is an incredibly useful app that allows you to see the location of all of your Apple devices on a map. You can remotely play sounds on devices (to help you find them under a pile of laundry, for example), send messages to them, and remotely erase them in case of theft. Of course, the app that's installed on your iPad won't help you find your iPad, but if your tablet goes missing and you don't have any other Apple devices, just log on to icloud.com to see where your device has wandered to.

Wrap Up

Whew! That wraps up the preinstalled apps on your iPad running iOS 9. If you think that's enough to keep you busy for a while, we certainly understand. You've probably also noticed that these apps are hardly self-contained - it seems like every app interacts with another app to provide the kind of unified, intuitive experience Apple is famous for.

As you move into the world of third party apps, you'll find that a large number of apps make use of your Contacts, Camera, Photos, Calendar, etc. In fact, in the next chapter, we'll set up Facebook, Twitter and Flickr, all of which can be deeply integrated into iOS 9 and all its functionality. If you're just starting out with your iPad, it's a good idea to be sure you understand these twenty-two preinstalled apps before you start downloading more – it'll give you a solid foundation not only for using new apps, but for understanding how they work.

Part 4: Making It Your Own: Customization

Getting your iPad set up just the way you like it is one of the more fun aspects of new iPad ownership. We've already discussed arranging your apps on your home screen and creating folders, and you've got an idea of how your apps work. Now let's take a look at other settings and personalization options available to you.

Most of this section will deal with your Settings area. You can access Settings from your home screen by tapping the Settings icon. You'll find Settings to be incredibly easy to navigate. You'll choose a subject from the left menu and tap it to see available options. Everything is exactly where you'd expect it to be, for the most part. And if you can't find something, be sure to check Settings > General, where odds and ends tend to hide out, or use the new Settings search bar at the top of the Settings app – a great new iOS 9 feature!

Screenshot 88: The Settings Menu

Tip: The Settings icon isn't the only graphic that uses gears. In plenty of apps, you can access additional settings by tapping gear icons.

4.1 Do Not Disturb Mode

Do Not Disturb mode is a handy feature located near the top of your settings app. When this operational mode is enabled, you won't receive any notifications and all of your FaceTime calls and incoming messages will be silenced. This is a useful trick for those times when you can't afford to be distracted (and let's face it, your iPad is as communicative as they come, and sometimes you'll need to have some peace and quiet!). Clock alarms **will** still sound.

To turn on, schedule and customize Do Not Disturb, just tap on Do Not Disturb in Settings. You can schedule automatic times to activate this feature, like your work hours, for example. You can also specify certain contacts that should be allowed when your tablet is set to Do Not Disturb. This way, your mother can still get through if she FaceTimes you, but you won't have to hear every incoming email. To do this, use the Allow Calls From command in Do Not Disturb settings.

Do Not Disturb is also accessible through the Control Center (swipe up from the bottom of the screen to access it at any time).

4.2 Notifications and Widgets

Notifications are one of the most useful features on the iPad, but chances are you won't need to be informed of every single event that's set as a default in your Notifications Center. To adjust Notifications preferences, go to Settings > Notifications.

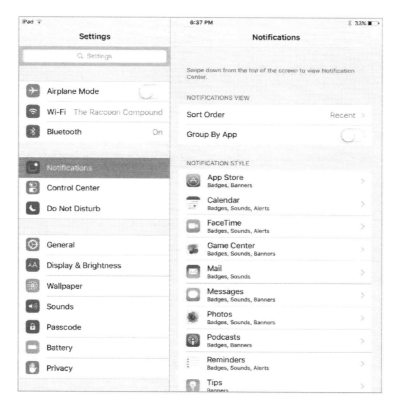

Screenshot 89: Notifications Settings

You can choose how you'd like your notifications sorted (manually or by time). You'll also see a list of all of the apps currently in the Notifications Center. By tapping the app, you can turn Notifications off or on and finesse the type of notification from each app. It's a good idea to whittle this list down to the apps that you truly want to be notified from. Reducing the number of sounds your iPad makes can also reduce iOS-related frazzledness. For example, in Mail, you may want your tablets to make a sound when you receive email from someone on your VIP list but to only display badges for other, less important email.

You can choose how you'd like your notifications sorted (manually or by time). iOS 9 defaults to grouping your notifications by date, though you can enable Group by App if you prefer the old arrangement. You'll also see a list of all of the apps currently in your Notifications Center. By tapping the app, you can turn Notifications off or on and finesse the type of notification from each app. It's a good idea to whittle this list down to the apps that you truly want to be notified from. For example, in Mail, you may want your iPad to make a sound when you receive email from someone on your VIP list but to only display badges for other, less important email.

Screenshot 90: Mail Notification Settings

You can also customize the widgets that appear in the Notifications Today panel. To do this, open Notifications by swiping down from the top of the screen. At the bottom of the Notifications Today tab, tap Edit. From there, you can remove widgets or add new ones. Note that widgets are now open to third party developers, so some of your favorite apps, like Evernote, may include widget versions. They will automatically appear under the Do Not Include heading in the Today Edit screen. To enable them, tap the green plus sign. We highly recommend installing the PCalc app (6.4) and enabling its widget!

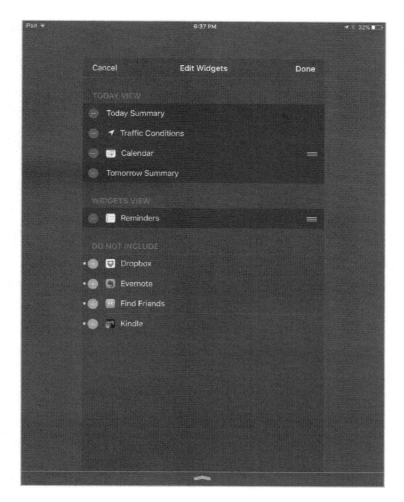

Screenshot 91: Customizing Widgets

4.3 General Settings

The General menu item is a little bit of a catchall. This is where you'll find information about your iPad, including its current version of iOS and any available software updates. Fortunately, iOS 9 ushers in an era of smaller, more efficient updates, so you won't find yourself scrambling to delete apps in order to make space for the latest improvements. You can also check your iPad and iCloud storage here.

This is also where you can adjust some of the decisions you made when you set up your iPad way back in 1.6. You can turn Siri on or off, or change its gender, set the date and time and set international options (like language and region).

The Accessibility options are located here as well. You can set your iPad according to your needs with Zoom, Voiceover, large text, color adjustment, and more. There are a quite a few Accessibility options that can make iOS 9 easy for everyone to use, including Grayscale View and improved Zoom options.

Screenshot 92: General Settings Menu

A very handy Accessibility option that's a little disguised is the Assistive Touch setting. This gives you a menu that helps you access device-level functions. Enabling it brings up a floating menu designed to help users who have difficulty with screen gestures like swiping or with manipulating the iPad's physical buttons.

We recommend taking some time and tapping through the General area, just so you know where everything is.

4.4 Battery

The new Battery heading in your Settings gives you really useful information about your device's battery usage. This is where you can enable the all-new Low Power mode to preserve battery life. You can also see which apps are using the highest percentage of your battery. Tap the clock icon to see how much time you've spent in each app to help you understand exactly how battery-hungry any given app is (and how much of your life each app is controlling!). For more tips on preserving battery life, skip ahead to 5.1.

Screenshot 93: Battery

4.5 Sound Preferences

Your iPad is a pretty talkative critter. You'll hear sounds for calendar and reminders, incoming emails, and more. Fortunately, you've got a lot of control over all those beeps, bells and whistles in Settings > Sounds. Be sure to try out the other sounds in iOS 9. If you had your heart set on a classic iPad sound, don't worry. They're all safely archived in the Classic folder.

4.6 Customizing iPad's Wallpaper

On the iPad, wallpaper refers to the background image on your home screen and to the image displayed when your iPad is locked (lock screen). You can change either image two ways.

For the first method, visit Settings > Wallpapers. Tap Choose a New Wallpaper. From there, you can choose a pre-loaded dynamic (moving) or still image, or choose one of your own photos. Once you've chosen an image, you'll see a preview of the image as a lock screen. Here, you can turn off Perspective Zoom, which makes the image appear to shift as you tilt your tablet) if you like. Tap Set Lock Screen, Set Home Screen or Set Both to continue.

Screenshot 94: Setting a Photo as Wallpaper

The other way to make the change is through your Photo app or through Photo Booth. Find the photo you'd like to set as a wallpaper image and tap the Share button. You'll be given a choice to set an image as a background, a lock screen, or both.

If you want to use images from the web, it's fairly easy. Just press and hold the image until the Save Image / Copy / Cancel message comes up. Saving the image will save it to your camera roll in the Photos app.

4.7 Privacy

The Privacy heading in Settings lets you know what apps are doing with your data. Every app you've allowed to use Location Services will show up under Location Services (and you can toggle Location Services off and on for individual apps or for your whole device). You can also go through all of your apps to see where information is going.

4.8 iCloud Settings

You can adjust what features are iCloud-enabled and what features aren't in the iCloud settings page. This may be useful if you have your own iPhone, but share your iPad with other family members and don't want to enable your iCloud mail on the shared device. You can also manage your iCloud backup settings here and keep track of friends and family with whom you've shared your location. You'll also find a heading for iCloud Drive here where you can enable the iCloud Drive app if you like. For more on iCloud Drive, see 4.14.

4.9 Mail, Contacts and Calendars Settings

If you need to add additional mail, contacts or calendar accounts, tap Settings > Mail, Contacts and Calendars to do so. It's more or less the same process as adding a new account in-app. You can also adjust other settings here, including your email signature for each linked account. This is also a good place to check which aspects of each account are linked – for example, you may want to link your Tasks, Calendars and Mail from Exchange, but not your Contacts. You can manage all of this here.

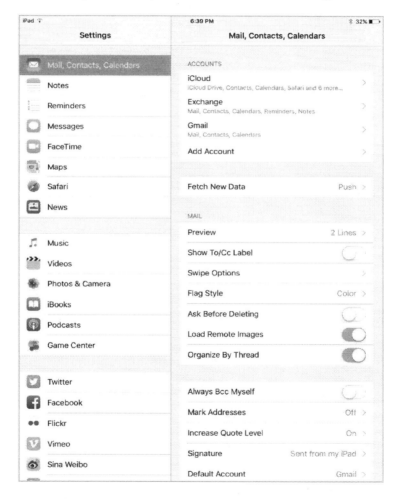

Screenshot 95: Mail, Contacts and Calendars Settings

There are a number of other useful settings here, including the frequency you want your accounts to check for mail (Push, the default, being the hardest on your battery life). You can also turn on features like Ask Before Deleting and adjust the day of the week you'd like your calendar to start on.

4.10 Miscellaneous App Settings

Many apps will show up in your Settings menu with various options. For example, this is where you can clear Safari's browser history, disable FaceTime, toggle Read Receipts in Messages, etc. We recommend taking some time to go through each app to see what you can do here. You can also sign in and out of the iTunes and App Stores here.

4.11 Adding Twitter, Facebook, Flickr and Vimeo Accounts

Screenshot 96: Integrating a Facebook Account

If you use Twitter, Facebook, Flickr or Vimeo, you'll probably want to integrate them with your iPad. This is a snap to do. Just tap on Settings, and look for the social networks list in the left menu. Tap on the platform you want to integrate. From there, you'll enter your user name and password. Doing this will allow you to share webpages, photos, notes, App Store pages, music and more directly from your iPad apps to your social network accounts.

iPad will ask you if you'd like to download each network's free app when you configure your account. We recommend doing this – the apps are easy to use, free, and look great on iPad.

We found that when we associated our Facebook accounts, our contact list got extremely bloated. If you don't want to include your Facebook friends in your contacts list, adjust the list of applications that can access your account.

4.12 Resetting Your iPad

If you're looking for the big red emergency button, this is it. In Settings > General > Reset, you'll find the options to reset all of your iPad's settings or to erase all content and settings (restore to factory settings). Less drastic options include a network reset, resetting the dictionary, resetting the home screen, and resetting location and privacy settings. These options are extremely useful when something goes wrong, but remember that any data lost during a reset cannot be recovered, so proceed with caution!

4.13 Family Sharing

Family Sharing is one of our favorite iOS 9 features. Family Sharing allows you to share App Store and iTunes purchases with family members (previously, accomplishing this required a tricky and not-entirely-in-compliance-with-terms-of-service dance). Turning on Family Sharing also creates a shared family calendar, photo album, and reminder list. Family members can also see each other's location in Apple's free Find My Friends app and check the location of each other's devices in the Find iPhone app. Overall, Family Sharing is a great way to keep everyone entertained and in sync. You can include up to six people in Family Sharing.

To enable Family Sharing, go to Settings > iCloud. Here, tap Set Up Family Sharing to get started. The person who initiates Family Sharing for a family is known as the family organizer. It's an important role, since every purchase made by family members will be made using the family organizer's credit card. Once you set up your family, they'll also be able to download your past purchases, including music, movies, books, and apps.

Invite your family members to join Family Sharing by entering their Apple IDs. As a parent, you can create Apple IDs for your children with parental consent. When you create a new child Apple ID, it is automatically added to Family Sharing.

There are two types of accounts in Family Sharing — adult and child. As you'd expect, child accounts have more potential restrictions than adult accounts do. Of special interest is the Ask to Buy option. This prevents younger family members from running up the family organizer's credit card bill by requiring parental authorization for purchases. The family organizer can also designate other adults in the family as capable of authorizing purchases on children's devices.

If you'd like to further lock down your children's iOS devices, be sure to take a look at 5.2 for information about setting up additional restrictions.

4.14 iCloud Drive

iCloud Drive is a cloud storage solution similar to Dropbox, and it's better than ever in iOS 9. iCloud Drive offers wireless file sharing and syncing between compatible devices. iCloud Drive support is built into OSX Yosemite and newer, but it won't work with earlier versions of Mac OSX. iCloud Drive will share files from your apps, including the iWork Suite, as well as any other file type used on your computer. You can monitor which apps are sharing files with iCloud Drive in Settings > iCloud > iCloud Drive.

Screenshot 97: iCloud Drive Settings

iOS 9 includes a full iCloud Drive app, though it's a bit hidden in the interface. Head to the iCloud Drive settings to enable it by turning on Show on Home Screen. This is a huge leap forward for iOS, which has never had anything resembling a file browser before. In the iCloud Drive app, you'll find all of your stored files in one place. Tap on them to open them in the appropriate app.

4.15 Continuity and Handoff

iOS 9 includes some incredible features for those of us who work on multiple iOS 9 and Yosemite OSX and newer devices. Now, when your computer is running Yosemite or higher or your iOS 9 iPad is connected to the same Wi-Fi network as your iOS 9 iPhone, you can answer calls or send text messages (both iMessages and regular SMS messages) from your iPad or computer.

The Handoff feature is present in apps like Numbers, Safari, Mail and many more. Handoff allows you to leave an app in one device mid-action and pick up right where you left off on a different device. It makes life much easier for those of us living a multi-gadget lifestyle.

Wrap Up

We've covered some of the more common personalization and customization options available in the Settings area. However, there are many more options and settings to explore. Before you move on, take a few minutes and go through the Settings menu item by item, just to see what's there. This is a great way to really take control of your iPad – even if you don't change anything, knowing your options will go a long way toward making you an iPad expert.

Part 5: Maintenance and Security

Now that you've spent so much time learning how to use your iPad and how to set it up to perfectly suit your needs, you'll want to be sure that all that effort won't go to waste. This chapter will share some tips for keeping your iPad safe from harm.

5.1 Maintenance

iPad requires very little maintenance, but there are a few things you can do to keep it happy and healthy.

Cleaning

It's a good idea to clean your iPad fairly regularly to keep your screen clear and the touchscreen functioning. The iPad screen is oleophobic, meaning it resists fingerprints, but you'll find it tends to get a little smudged. Excessive grime can also interfere with the touchscreen's responsiveness.

Use a microfiber cloth and specialized screen cleaning fluid (NOT other household cleaners or water) to gently wipe the screen every so often.

Case

iPad is fairly tough, but not indestructible. It's also not cheap. It's a good idea to find a case to help protect it from falls. You can find cases like Apple's Smart Cover that automatically wake the iPad up when opened. Many also fold into stands to help prop up your iPad, and some include Bluetooth keyboards. There are plenty of cases out there for every budget and lifestyle, and we strongly recommend finding one that works best for you.

Battery

Nothing puts a damper on an iPad work session quicker than having to scramble for a source of power. While the iPad has an amazing 10-hour battery life, if you'll be away from a power source for an extended period of time (such as an international plane flight), follow these tips to make the battery last as long as possible.

Battery Basics

"Battery life" refers to the amount of time your iPad will run before it must be recharged. While your iPad may have a battery life of 10 hours, if you frequently run a lot of energy-hogging applications, you'll find that your iPad does not last a full 10 hours in between charges. To help your battery life last, be sure to put your iPad into lock mode when you are not using it, and get in the habit of charging it often. Plugging the iPad into a wall will charge it much faster than merely charging through a computer's USB port. In fact, leaving it plugged in to a hibernating computer may actually drain the battery.

Use it (up) or lose it

Every few weeks, it's a good idea to let your battery drain all the way to the bottom of its charge. This keeps your iPad from giving you inaccurate reads on remaining battery life.

Update, Update, Update!

Keep your iPad system updated to the latest software version, and keep your apps updated as well. While the app content and user interface may not change, app updates often improve performance and battery usage. So don't be lazy – keep your apps up to date!

Settings

If you have the ability to regularly charge your iPad, you may not worry about getting a full 10 hours out of the iPad's battery life. However, if you have limited access to power sources, making a few tweaks to settings or disabling unnecessary apps will reduce your iPad's energy consumption and help maximize battery life.

- Airplane Mode: Use this mode, which turns off your Wi-Fi and 3G, whenever you don't need those functions to be active. Go to Settings -> Airplane Mode -> On or swipe up from the bottom of the screen to reveal Control Center. Your iPad uses battery life to connect to Wi-Fi and 3G, and the weaker the connection, the more battery life it can end up using to keep that connection active (or to search for a signal if the connection is lost).

- Push notifications and fetch data: Some applications use push notifications to send alerts or frequently fetch data (for example: Facebook, Mail). The more frequently data is fetched or push notifications sent, the faster your battery may drain, as this uses energy to continually update. Changing your fetch settings to every hour or to manual only (rather than every few minutes) reduces energy consumption. This setting will be located in Settings > [App Name].

- Minimize Location Services: Applications that use locations services will drain the battery faster. To reduce consumption, go to Settings > General > Location Services and use location services only when needed.

- Dim it down and keep it cool: You can change brightness to a lower setting — in Settings > "Brightness and Wallpaper." Using only as much brightness as you need will help your battery last longer. It will also keep your battery from overheating.

- Don't auto check your mail: Under regular circumstances, your mail accounts may be set to auto check for new mail every few minutes and download new messages. Turn off auto check in Settings > Mail, Contacts, Calendars > Fetch New Data to preserve battery life. Messages will now be downloaded by your iPad only when you check for them, rather than automatically.

- Turn off or minimize background app refresh: Turning off or at least reducing background app refresh is a really good idea, especially for users with older iPads. Multitasking is great, but if you don't need it, you'll definitely feel its effects on your battery. It's a simple fix, though – just go to Settings > General > Background App Refresh to turn it off altogether or turn it off app by app.

- Monitor your apps: iOS 9 lets you see exactly which apps are draining your battery the most. Visit Settings > General > Usage > Battery Usage to see which apps have consumed the largest percentage of your battery life over either the last 24 hours or over the last seven days. When your battery's running low, you can use this information to help it last a little longer by avoiding your really power-hungry apps.

Temperature

Like humans, the iPad *can* function in temperatures ranging from 32 to 95 degrees Fahrenheit, but it's happiest at 72 degrees (room temperature). Be very careful with extreme heat and cold; they can ruin your iPad if you're not careful. Be especially careful about leaving your device in the car – if it's too hot to leave a baby or a dog in a vehicle, don't leave your iPad in one either!

5.2 Security

There are a few things you can do to help secure your iPad, and iOS 9 includes serious improvements in security. Setting up Find My iPad during setup is a good start, but if you need to further secure your device, here are four other powerful options.

Setting a Passcode

To set a passcode that must be entered every time your iPad turns on or wakes up (if you haven't already during the initial setup process), go to Settings > Touch ID & Passcode. Tap Turn Passcode On and enter a four-digit password of your choosing.

iPad defaults to a simple passcode of four numbers. However, you can access more options by tapping More Passcode Options. You can expand the passcode to six digits if you like, or if you're really cautious, use a custom alphanumeric code (letters and numbers). This will give you more leeway in designing your passcode. You can also set your iPad to erase all of its data if more than ten incorrect passcodes are entered – do NOT do this if you're unsure about your ability to remember your passcode!

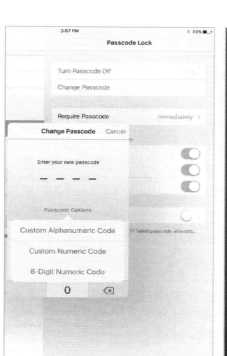

Screenshot 98: Setting and Using a Passcode

Touch ID (Fingerprint Sensing)

The iPad Air 2 was the first iPad model to come pre-equipped with a fingerprint scanner integrated into the enlarged Home button on the device and you'll find it on the iPad Pro and iPad Mini for as well. This means that you can set up your own unique fingerprint as a password for your iPad. Simply pressing the Home button will authenticate you and unlock the tablet in one nearly impossible to hack motion. You can also use this feature to authenticate App Store and iTunes purchases – no more poking out your Apple ID password!

Touch ID is easy to set up, if you skipped this step during the initial setup process. Visit Settings > Touch ID & Passcode. Tap Add a Fingerprint and follow the instructions to set up your own unique fingerprint. The more often you use it, the more accurate it gets! We recommend adding multiple fingers, as you can add more than one print to your iPad.

Restrictions

Restrictions are useful settings for parents worried about their children's ability to run up the family credit card or for parents who want to control their child's access to certain features, like the Camera. To set restrictions, visit Settings > General > Restrictions.

Tap "Enable Restrictions" to get started. You'll be prompted for a four-digit restrictions passcode. After you set that up, you'll be able to prevent subsequent iPad users from using Safari, iTunes, FaceTime, or any of the other apps listed in the Restrictions settings area. You can also filter for explicit language, allow or disallow in-app purchases, and set acceptable ratings for viewable content (e.g. movies with PG ratings). Parents can even set an audio volume limit to protect developing eardrums! We strongly recommend that parents and educators familiarize themselves with restrictions, for the well being of their children and their bank accounts.

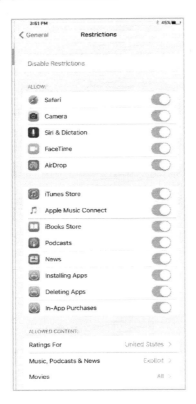 

Screenshot 99: Restrictions

Guided Access

Guided Access may be useful for parents or educators who want to limit iPad use to a single app. To use it, first you'll need to turn it on in Settings > General > Accessibility > Guided Access. After enabling Guided Access, tapping the Home button three times while in the app you want to limit the user to will activate Guided Access mode. You can set time limits in Guided Access as well, forcing the user to end his or her session after a duration of your choosing.

Wrap Up

It's easy to forget how much of a financial investment your iPad is, since you'll probably carry it with you everywhere. However, as convenient and easy to use as iPad is, it remains a highly sophisticated and fairly expensive electronic device, and you'll want to follow the suggestions outlined above to keep it safe. We also cannot stress the importance of security enough. iPads get lost or worse, stolen, very frequently. Chances are, you'll load your own tablet up with highly personal information that you'll want to safeguard should your iPad fall into the wrong hands. Fortunately, thanks to the security features discussed above, it's easy to configure your device so that a thief won't be able to make off with much besides a tablet-shaped paperweight!

Part 6: Must-Have Apps for Your iPad

You've no doubt heard Apple's catch phrase, "there's an app for that." And it's usually true! This section outlines some of our favorite apps, though with well over one million apps available in the iPad App Store, you're bound to discover hidden gems we haven't covered here.

Note: all prices are current as of November 2015. However, like anything related to finances, they are subject to change.

6.1 Games

If you enjoy games, then you have chosen the right tablet! Here are some of our favorites, but be warned: some of these pose a serious risk to your work, school, and sleep.

2048 (Free)

We feel irresponsible even recommending this one, it's so absurdly addictive. It's a tile game whose goal is to create the number 2048 by doubling the numbers on tiles by matching them with each other. Don't say we didn't warn you.

Alto's Adventure ($2.99)

This snowy, tranquil game consists of an endless snowboarding challenge, and its beautiful flat graphics and soothing soundtrack make for a very peaceful gaming experience. It's not as challenging as many of the games on this list, but it's satisfying to play and gorgeous to look at.

Angry Birds (Full version: $2.99 / Lite version: Free)

Angry Birds is a classic iPad app that has helplessly addicted players for years. Game play is deceptively simple – launch a bird from a slingshot and cause enough destruction to vanquish the evil green pigs. However, as you progress through the levels, you'll find yourself faced with increasingly difficult physics challenges. The game is available in a number of editions, including Angry Birds Seasons and Angry Birds Space.

Clash of Clans (Free)

Build your village, improve it by raiding other players' villages for resources, defend it from marauding players, and team up with others by joining a clan! This is a free, social game with in-app purchases.

Contre Jour ($2.99)

This is worth playing for the artwork alone. Use your finger to alter the ground the one-eyed spherical protagonist rolls across to reach a blue light. Lovely game.

Crossy Road (free, in-app purchases)

Crossy Road is an upsettingly addictive little game in which your simple objective is to get across the road before the bottom of the screen catches up with you. Unfortunately, the road's a dangerous place, full of traffic and other obstacles that your mascot (a chicken, a duck, a horse, etc.) must avoid. You can't wait too long to cross, though, because the screen is constantly scrolling upward, and if you can't keep up, you'll be lunch for the hawks. It's incredibly similar to Frogger, and it's easy to lose entire afternoons to this one.

Fruit Ninja (Full version: $0.99 / Lite version: Free)

Use your finger to slice fruit with your ninja sword, best your high scores, and compete with friends. We couldn't tell you why this is so much fun, but trust us, it is.

Monument Valley ($3.99)

Journey through a gorgeously designed M.C. Escher- esque world, solving puzzles that defy our understanding of space. Perfect for all ages.

Plants Versus Zombies ($0.99)

This wildly creative twist on tower defense pits weaponized botany against the undead. It's a winning and highly addictive mix of grotesque cuteness, strategy, and quick thinking. Highly recommended!

Plants versus Zombies 2: It's About Time (Free)

The blockbuster original Plants versus Zombies game returns in this sequel for FREE, with in-app purchases. Built on a classic tower defense gameplay model, PVZ adds bizarre and hilarious characters as the player pits weaponized botany against legions of the undead. This sequel adds a time travel component that results in maps in Ancient Egypt, a pirate ship, and the Old West for starters.

The Room ($0.99) / The Room 2 ($1.99) / The Room 3 ($4.99)

These extremely atmospheric puzzle games consist of a variety of geometric, physical and logical puzzles centered on mysterious boxes and other objects in a series of increasingly strange rooms. These games are hideously addictive, but the spooky ambiance might be a bit too much for very young players.

6.2 Reading and News Apps

In addition to News and iBooks, you can download several apps that expand the reading material available on iPad.

Comixology (Free)

If you're a comic book fan, this is an essential app. Its Guided View feature lets you move from panel to panel naturally. The app is free, but the comics usually cost money. Set up an account with Comixology to buy comics at the Comixology website and then read them using this app. It's easy and impressively close to reading a dead tree comic. The selection is reasonable, and includes Marvel, DC, Vertigo and Image titles, among others.

Flipboard (Free)

Flipboard presents your Facebook, Twitter, Tumblr, Sound Cloud and other content in a beautiful magazine layout. It's a great way to consolidate your information feeds into one aesthetically pleasing interface that's perfect for flipping through.

Nook (Free)

Turn your iPad into a Nook ereader with the Nook app from Barnes and Noble. Sign in with your Barnes and Noble account to have Nook books wirelessly delivered to your iPad. It's easy to use and the Nook library is huge.

Kindle (Free)

The Kindle app will allow you to download ebooks from Amazon's Kindle store.

NPR (Free)

The magazine-style user interface of this app emphasizes news, arts, lifestyle and music coverage. You can access hundreds of NPR live stations (searchable by GPS or ZIP code) and on-demand broadcast streams, and create a playlist of stories to save for later. Enjoy stunning photojournalism with full-page zoom, and share stories via e-mail, Twitter and Facebook.

Overdrive Media Console (Free)

Check with your local public library to see if it subscribes to Overdrive Media. If so, this free app will let you download free library ebooks and audiobooks to your iPad.

Reuters News Pro (Free)

This app puts you at the pulse of Reuter's venerable newswire. Customize your daily feed by choosing from dozens of categories, create a specific list for business news, and further customize with geographic-specific newsfeeds.

The Weather Channel (Free)

If you're a weather junkie, definitely install the official Weather Channel app. It's a beautiful and easy-to-use HD experience.

Dark Sky ($3.99)

This award-winning ultra-local weather app lets you know with amazing specificity exactly when it's going to rain at your precise location. If you find yourself squinting at the radar map, try this one. It's scarily good at what it does.

6.3 Music, TV and Movies

Fandango (Free)

This Wallet-ready app will help you find movies near you and purchase tickets.

Flixter (Free)

Movie lovers will want Flixter, which includes reviews from Rotten Tomatoes and finds movie theaters near you, along with show times, trailers and more.

Hulu Plus (Free)

If you have a Hulu Plus account, you'll want access on your iPad. The app is free to install, but the actual Hulu Plus subscription is paid.

Netflix (Free)

If you subscribe to Netflix, this is an essential app! The iPad is perfect for streaming movies, and the Netflix app is easy to use. Just sign in with your account and start watching.

Pandora (Free)

The pioneer of Internet radio is now available at a flick of your fingertips. The user interface also features a few improvements over the existing computer version; it displays a sliding panel of albums, your playlists, and detailed artist info as each track plays. If you've already got a Pandora account set up, you'll want to install the app to gain access to your stations. Otherwise, you might as well just use iTunes Radio.

Spotify (Free, paid subscription optional)

Spotify is another streaming music service that's worth your attention. You can play any artist, album or playlist you like, for free.

6.4 Productivity

Dropbox (Free)

Dropbox is a useful tool for moving files from computer to computer, especially if one of those computers is a Windows computer. Install the free app, register for a free Dropbox account, and you're ready to take advantage of very easy-to-use cloud storage. You can also install the Dropbox program on your computer, or just head to Dropbox.com to access your files from any Internet connection. Dropbox is also a great way to transfer photos from your iPad to a non-Apple environment. Highly recommended.

Evernote (Free)

Change the way you take notes; never forget an important message or an unexpected, special moment. Turn snippets from blogs, recorded sounds and graphic images or photos into digital notes. Take advantage of the iPad's near life-size keyboard to type a quick message. View and access all your notes with a few swipes of your finger, quickly find the notes you need with 'tag' view, and use the map to geo-tag your notes. Syncs automatically over a Wi-Fi or 3G connection with your desktop Evernote and your smart phone Evernote.

Google Chrome (Free)

Safari has greatly improved in iOS 9, but if you're too deeply entangled in Google's browser, you'll be able to access your stored Google data and other Chrome-y goodness on your iPad as well.

LastPass (Free with a paid LastPass subscription)
LastPass with Safari and Touch ID integration is a miracle in this age of high-profile password hacks. LastPass is a password manager and it's one of the finest around. With LastPass Premium you get access to the LastPass iOS app and Safari browser extension. Imagine only needing to remember one password while maintaining extremely secure and unique passwords for every single account in your life. We can't recommend this one enough, and at $12 a year, it's not unreasonably priced.

PCalc Lite / Calculator FREE (Free)

For some reason, iPad doesn't ship with a native calculator. You will in all likelihood want one, though, and here are two reasonable options. We tend to prefer PCalc Lite, since it has more functionality, but if you just want a bare bones calculator for basic math, Calculator FREE is less cluttered.

Wunderlist (Free)
If you're a serious list maker, you'll want to install this free cloud-based list system. Wunderlist gives you serious flexibility and collaboration options, making it a beefier, cross-platform-compatible alternative to your iPad's Notes and Reminders apps.

6.5 Education
Educators realized the iPad's potential as a learning tool early on, and you can reap the benefits with these educational apps!

DuoLingo (Free)
DuoLingo is a language-learning app that game-ifies language acquisition. It's fun and easy and a great way to get started with a foreign language.

Google Earth (Free)
Google Earth is a highly accurate virtual map and so much more! As a digital globe, it allows you to not only zoom in on specific places, but you can also take 3D tours of entire cities. In recent versions, you can even take 3D virtual tours of museums, monuments, and other landmarks. In recent versions, you can even explore the bottom of the ocean and the surface of Mars. Google Earth is a must-have app for your iPad.

Google Translate (Free)

The Google Translate app is wonderful for traveling or language study. Of course, you can't rely on it to construct sentences that don't sound machine-translated, but it's a great quick way to look up a word in a foreign language on the fly.

Star Walk ($2.99)

This app is a good choice for demonstrating the awesomeness of the iPad. Use it to view the labeled night sky. Location Services allow you to point your tablet in any direction (including down) to see what's going on in the galaxy. The 360-degree view of the universe is breathtaking. If you're only going to buy one app, we can't recommend this one enough.

Wikipanion (Free)

This app puts the world's collective knowledge at your fingertips, distilling Wikipedia's content into an iPad-friendly viewing pane and easy-to-use interface. Save images you find to your iPad's photo library and bookmark your favorite searches. If you truly love the app, you may want to upgrade to the Plus version for $2.99; you'll enjoy faster page load speeds and will be able to save pages for offline reading at a later time.

6.6 Creative Tools

Adobe Vector Draw (Free)

Your new digital sketchbook allows you to capture and explore ideas no matter where you are when inspiration strikes. Combining classic elements from Adobe Photoshop and Illustrator, such as layers, brushes, and undo/redo, Adobe Vector Draw (which replaced Adobe Ideas) upgrades your drawings from pixilated scribbles to artistic sketches. The best part? No graphic design background is required!

Epicurious (Free)

The premier app for foodies, the easy-to-use interface turns your iPad into a luxury cookbook featuring over 30,000 recipes. Save favorite recipes, add ingredients to a shopping list, and search for recipes by main ingredients, course, cuisine, dietary restrictions, season and occasion. With gorgeous graphics, you may find yourself drooling over the amazing dishes!

Photoshop Express (Free)

This is a very, very abbreviated version of Adobe's famous photo editing software, but it will allow you to do some basic fixes that you can't do in the Photos app.

Penultimate (Free)

The best-selling handwriting app for iPad allows you to take notes and draft sketches.

ScreenChomp (Free)

ScreenChomp is a free screencasting app. Record doodles, sketches, and more. Fun and easy to use!

6.7 Social Media

Skype (Free)

The Skype app is a great alternative to FaceTime if you have friends and family who haven't jumped on the Apple bandwagon (yet). Skype video calls are just as free and just as high quality as their FaceTime counterparts.

Snapchat (Free)

Snapchat has a bit of an image problem, due to well-publicized illicit uses for this fun disposable messaging app, but it's actually quite a bit of fun to use for innocuous purposes. Snapchat messages self-destruct after viewing, making it a silly and fun way to share short video bursts without running up anybody's storage use. We should stress though that Snapchat is not particularly secure and anything you send using it could be reproduced as a screenshot or screencast.

WordPress (Free)

Create, save and publish posts and pages for your WordPress blog directly from your iPad.

Yelp (Free)

Check local reviews wherever you go for advice on restaurants, activities and services. Search for a specific business or general service; check hours and narrow search results by neighborhood, price and distance.

Pinterest, Facebook, Twitter, YouTube, Vimeo, et al. (Generally Free)

Most major online platforms include a free app, which typically provides a much richer experience than what's available in a mobile browser. If there's a service you find yourself using daily, check the App Store to see if there's an appified version!

6.8 Lifestyle

Kayak (Free)

Quickly search across most major airlines for airfare prices, with a simple interface for picking start/end dates, destination and a date range. Set up airfare price alerts and be notified when fares drop.

MyFitnessPal (Free)

MyFitnessPal is an excellent calorie counter app that makes watching what you eat painless (er, relatively painless). You can search for most foods to automatically add nutritional information or simply scan barcodes. Add your calories burned through exercise and stay on track to meet your weight loss and/or health goals.

ShopStyle (Free)

ShopStyle is an elegant shopping app that includes over 300 retailers. Fun to use, and potentially very dangerous if you're trying to not to spend money.

Shpock (Free)

If you like garage sales and classified ads, run don't walk to download this sale finder app.

Trulia (Free)

Find your dream home with Trulia's real estate finder for iPad. Search by location, save searches, view photos, reviews, and more. A must-have app for anyone looking for a home.

Wrap Up

We hope these apps have given you some ideas for using your iPad! If none of the above caught your fancy, think about what you enjoy. Try finding it in the App Store – there are apps for musicians, writers, computer programmers, parents, etc., and there's bound to be something just for you!

Conclusion

By now, you should be ready to use your new iPad like a pro. You know how to get around and make the most of your preinstalled apps, how to customize your settings, how to take care of your iPad, and how to find new apps to help you get the most out of iPad and iOS 9.

We hope you've enjoyed getting to know your iPad. There's so much more to explore, though, and as you become more familiar with your device, you'll discover new and exciting ways to use it that we've never even dreamed of. Those possibilities are just part of the fun of owning an iOS device. As you continue to use your iPad, you'll find ways to adapt it to your unique personality and lifestyle. With the information in this guide, you now have a solid foundation to build on, and we hope your iPad brings you years of entertainment, education, productivity and usefulness.

Good luck and have fun!

Made in the USA
Charleston, SC
21 June 2016